My friends, Peter and Stephanie Chung, are faithful servants of the Lord. They have held on to their faith in times of suffering and hard times. They are the true definition of what good parents are. The couple brought up Joseph, who had autism, with love and strong faith in God. When God called Joseph home, Peter and Stephanie did not remain in grief over their son's tragic accident. They transformed it into a God-given vision to establish a social enterprise called Joe's Table. By hiring people with handicaps at the café, the couple opened windows of opportunities for them to take part as members of society. The story of their son, Joseph, in *Joe's Table* will provide deep comfort and healing to other parents around the globe.

—BILLY KIM, chairman,
Far East Broadcasting Company

Stephanie Chung's *Joe's Table*, which is about her and Peter's first son, Joseph, is a testimony to the love of a mother for a son who had attributes and gifts that surpassed those of others—gifts of love, joy, and encouragement—that far exceeded his capacities in other areas of life. What a joy to see how the Chung family was enhanced by each of their children! The truths of this life story will encourage and touch many families who share in this special pilgrimage of challenge and comfort, knowing that God loves them and in his special grace fulfills his loving plan and purpose.

—WILL GRAHAM, vice president,
Billy Graham Evangelistic Association

This deeply spiritual memoir about an extraordinary boy and a resilient and remarkable mother will offer hope to all who read this truly remarkable story. Stephanie's late son, Joseph, suffered from autism and seizure disorder throughout his life. Readers will experience Stephanie's heart-wrenching yet beautiful journey as a mother of a child with complicated health needs and be inspired by her profound spiritual transformation.

—JIM PATTISON, CEO and chairman of Jim Pattison Group

The Psalmist reminds us that God "prepares a table before us," even though we may be surrounded with formidable challenges. The words of Stephanie Chung in *Joe's Table* encourage our hearts as she shares with us how God can use the challenges of the challenged to bring light and hope to the shadows of our times. Her son, Joseph, was a shining example of the surprises God has in store if we allow Him to set the tables of our lives.

—HONORABLE STOCKWELL DAY, PC, ICDD

No mother in the world should have to bury her child. It is against the laws of nature. But such unspeakable tragedies happen. As a friend and spiritual sister of Dr. Stephanie Chung, I have come to understand the source of her strength and resilience to rise above the immeasurable pain of the loss of her first-born son. It is her faith in God, our Creator, who made Joseph in his own image and sent him into this world. Joseph is her angel and her inspiration in death as he was in life. By the grace of God, Joseph lived a life of joy and devotion while challenged with autism and seizures. Stephanie's courage, deep faith, and unbounded love for Joseph gave birth to this book, *Joe's Table*. And this book is her gift to you. May this book touch you deeply and bless you with the grace of God.

—The Honorable Yonah Martin, Canadian senator

As a child I sang the hymn "Faith Is the Victory," and I could not help but be reminded of that truth after reading Dr. Stephanie Chung's *Joe's Table*—a personal and touching story of sweet Joseph. This intimate history of a family's love and devotion to one so innocent and good is nothing short of inspirational. It is a must-read for parents in need of encouragement and for anyone else whose journey has left them lonely and even afraid. Stephanie Chung and her husband, Peter, shine a light for the rest of us.

—Andrew K. Benton, president and CEO,
Pepperdine University, Malibu, California

It has been a great honor for me to meet Stephanie and to have fellowship with her. When I see her encourage others and care for them as a wife, a mother, or a friend, I see Jesus. The love that she extends to everyone, even when she is going through a difficult time, gives us a glimpse of God's character. Her evident courage and passion has made a deep impression on me. Joseph's life has left us with beautiful and unforgettable memories that will remain with us and all who know this admirable family. *Joe's Table* will be a comfort and encouragement to those experiencing adversities in life, and it will bring all readers hope and peace. This book is like a beautiful song to our Lord who is vast and good.

—Maria Gloria Penayo de Duarte,
the former first lady of Paraguay

Joe's Table

A Place Where Disabilities Become Gifts

DR. STEPHANIE CHUNG

BroadStreet
PUBLISHING

BroadStreet Publishing Group, LLC
Racine, Wisconsin, USA
BroadStreetPublishing.com

Joe's Table: A Place Where Disabilities Become Gifts

Stock or custom editions of BroadStreet Publishing titles may be purchased in bulk for educational, business, ministry, fundraising, or sales promotional use. For information, please e-mail info@ broadstreetpublishing.com.

Cover design by Chris Garborg at garborgdesign.com.
Typesetting by Katherine Lloyd at theDESKonline.com.

Printed in the United States of America

18 19 20 21 22 5 4 3 2 1

Contents

Prologue

This book is the story of my family. It's also a confession of faith. My faith testifies to the presence of God, who works through every person's life.

To be honest, it wasn't easy for me to write about my firstborn son Joseph's life, cut short at thirty-two years. Even though I know Joseph was a true blessing and is now in God's kingdom, he will forever be buried in my heart.

Whenever I remember our time together—both the happy and the difficult moments—I am overcome with grief and pain. The sight of his bedroom, the letters he wrote, his handwritten book of the Bible's Psalms, and the photos of his smiling face make my yearning for him deeper and more desperate, and I can hardly control my emotions.

As I have re-created the moments with Joseph for this book, I have been pushed to depths of deep regret and elevated to heights of extreme gratitude. Ultimately, what compelled me to write this book is the unfailing love of God. Though Joseph's death was in God's plan, I relentlessly questioned him. I couldn't understand or accept it. Throughout this emotional journey, God's love was so sincere. He made me realize that he wanted me to testify of his amazing love, even with my immense sorrow.

My hope is that this book conveys the message of God, who has turned pain into victory through Joseph's life and death. This story has not yet ended; in fact, it should always be told in the present tense as a work in progress. That way, the story will be open-ended, just like God's infinite love. While writing this book, I rediscovered this verse: "Very truly I tell you, unless a kernel of wheat falls to the ground and dies, it remains only a single seed. But if it dies, it produces many seeds" (John 12:24). The symbolic meaning of this verse has resonated with me, especially during this time.

To my parents and my husband's parents, who have devoted their lives to pray persistently for our family: I am so grateful and moved to tears whenever I remember your love and sacrifice.

To my husband, who has shared every painful and joyful moment with me: I love you and admire you from the bottom of my heart.

To our four surviving children, Samuel, Hannah, Esther, and Christian, and our daughter-in-law Sujin: you are my fortresses of great blessing. I love you all. Special thanks to my daughter Esther, who translated my earlier Korean version of this book into English.

To the many great pastors who have supported my family and me: your faithful intercessory prayers have blessed and encouraged us.

To the beloved Bethesda mothers, who are now as close as blood relatives to me: your love strengthens me.

Prologue

■ □ ■ □ ■ □ ■ □ ■ □ ■ □ ■ □ ■ □ ■ □ ■ □ ■ □ ■ □ ■ □ ■ □ ■ □ ■ □ ■ □ ■

To Joseph's teachers, who helped him mature wonderfully: I will never forget your love and the sweat and tears you poured out for Joseph.

I extend my thanks to my editor, Bill Watkins, and publisher, BroadStreet Publishing Group, for their assistance. Without them, it would have been impossible for me to organize my thoughts and memories into a beautiful book.

Finally, to all those who are suffering now or are family and friends of those who are suffering: I pray you will be able to feel the living breath and tender touch of God in your lives through this small book.

Stephanie Chung
Vancouver, British Columbia, Canada

Three Questions

I t's a boy! Our first baby is a boy!"

A smile filled my husband's face as he gazed at our baby boy for the first time. His tiny little face looked just like his father's.

Most people cry when overwhelmed with happiness, but we couldn't stop laughing when we first met our son. An expression I've often heard is "It can only be a miracle if you're so overjoyed." If that is true, Joe's birth must have been a miracle. We laughed so hard the doctors in the delivery room thought we were nutty.

On June 23, 1980, our child came to us, carrying with him a happy melody like the prelude to a musical score. He came to us as if he were our greatest blessing and God's greatest gift. He illuminated all our faces with the light of his tiny but dazzling smile.

From that day on, our minds were filled with images of our

son's future. All parents hope for the best when bringing a child into the world, and I was no exception. I prayed our son's future would be filled with blessings from God. I knew life could also be full of harsh realities and unexpected misfortunes, but looking at my son, I believed somehow we would be exempt from such things. How could I have known of the unspeakable trial this bundle of joy would later bring?

This story is about the extraordinary time I spent with my son. He gave me the whole world and shook me to my very core. He drove me to my knees, hung me by a single thread, and left me no choice but to find answers in God. Our son could be like someone you meet today or tomorrow. Someone who may look weak and insignificant, but is in fact God's messenger.

Before I share Joe's story, here is some background about me. My father first heard the Gospel from missionaries when he was twenty years old and was instantly born again. From that point on, he devoted his life to church music, which, in the 1930s, was rare in Korea. He sang hymns, conducted the church choir, and played various instruments. He often said, "Life's purpose is to praise God."

My father's passion for music transferred to me, and at age five, I started piano lessons. From that point on, my passion for music and piano never ceased. My mother fully supported my music. "Your hands are to be used to praise God," she would say. "Be careful not to injure your hands!" I was not even allowed to wash dishes out of fear I could somehow damage my piano-playing hands.

Three Questions

■ ■

When I first met my husband-to-be, Moon Hyun (Peter) Chung, I was a music student who was several months away from graduating from university and a pianist at Suhyun Church in Seoul. He was a bachelor with an average salary who took a two-week vacation to find a wife in Korea.

At the time Peter journeyed to Korea in search of a wife, I was making plans to study abroad in America or Germany to pursue a master's degree in piano. "If you're going to go abroad to study, you must marry first! We will not send you by yourself," my father declared. I would have made further plans to go abroad had my father not been so fiercely against it. During this "battle" with my parents, our pastor gave them unexpected news after a Wednesday evening service. He told them a young Korean man from America was visiting our church to look for a future wife. Unknown to me, my pastor was trying to be our matchmaker.

"*Sungjaya* [my name when I am being addressed in Korean], you should at least meet him once," my mother said. Neither my parents nor I knew who this man was. Looking back, the fact that my parents wholeheartedly pushed me in the direction of a perfect stranger makes me think that our setup was simply God's plan.

"Not only is he a faithful man of God, his parents are faithful as well," my pastor added.

My parents were clearly enthused by our pastor's introduction. They had lived through hardship both during the Japanese occupation of Korea and during the Korean War. They'd concluded no certainty existed in life, except faith in God.

"Thanks for coming," Peter said as he approached us in the church's fellowship hall. "We don't have a lot of time. Let me cut to the chase and ask you three questions."

This is the first thing my suitor said to me when I met him. Beyond his blunt words, his Korean was awkward. He told me when he first immigrated to the United States at age fourteen, he spoke only Spanish and English every day. He was from California and had a dark tan, which I wasn't accustomed to seeing in Korea. On top of that, he spoke so earnestly and seriously with a deep *Gyungsangdo* (Southern Korean) accent that he seemed to be completely unaware of how odd he sounded to me.

"What do you believe is the purpose of life?" he asked.

His first question seemed rather inappropriate to ask a total stranger. But then I thought, *He must have sincere intentions to ask me this. He must have prayed and felt led by God in this search.* So I decided to answer the man who came all the way to Korea looking for a mate.

I remembered this question being asked during my Sunday school class when I was in junior high. So I replied, "You mean the goal of life? Isn't it to glorify God and attempt to please God with our lives?"

His face showed satisfaction.

"Thank you. I will now ask you my second question. I originally wanted to be a missionary, but I didn't become one. So I am asking …"

"Yes, go on."

"I would like to go into business so I can become someone who supports missionaries. I believe God will bless me financially. If that is the case, then I'd like to use my money for God's glory. What do you think about that?"

I was thinking, *This man is earning a meager salary. He just graduated from college a short while ago and has nothing to his name, except student loans.* For him to think he would be blessed with lots of money was pretty absurd. Yet he spoke with such conviction—it didn't feel as if he were saying something just to impress me. (Attempts to impress often happened during matchmaking meetings.) His unwavering conviction displayed the kind of faith that would not be shaken in the face of an unknown future. Peter asked his questions with such innocence, like a child trusting wholeheartedly in his parents to provide the right answers.

"If blessed financially, of course, one should live the way you describe," I answered. Perhaps he was pleased by the way I answered his question; he gazed at me momentarily, smiling.

I had no idea why he asked me these questions, but I understood once we got married.

〜

Peter's grandfather was imprisoned in Korea during the Japanese occupation for refusing to deny Christ and participate in Shintoism. He was tortured and beaten and then released in 1943. He was a pastor of a church in the southern part of South Korea in *Saamchunpo* in *Kyungsangnamdo*. After several lengthy prison sentences, he was thrown out of prison, wrapped in a straw sack and near death.

■ □ □ □ □ ■ □ □ □ □ □ ■ □ □ □ □ □ ■ □ □ □ □ □ ■ □ □ □ □ □ ■ □ □ □ □ □ ■

I also learned that my husband's father inherited an unshakable faith in God. He was a high school teacher who taught Korean literature but left Korea for America to pursue higher education. That way, he could return to Korea to teach at a university.

However, during his time in America, he felt a calling to become a pastor of a church. He started a church with five other Korean international students, building the church from the ground up, while experiencing a life of poverty and hardship. This was my father-in-law.

Apparently, Peter had a lot of issues as a teenager growing up in Los Angeles. He spent those years rebelling against his father. When his father started his church, there were no more than three thousand Koreans in the greater Los Angeles area. Peter couldn't understand his father's decision to build a small Korean church and walk that lonely road with little promise of any future. It also didn't make sense to him that a man with post-graduate level degrees would throw his future away, without hesitation, to start a church with no money.

More than anything, my husband couldn't stand watching his mother work at a sweatshop twelve hours a day just to support the family. He didn't understand his father's indifference to the family's financial state. He felt helpless watching his mother slowly deteriorate in health; she often held her bladder to avoid taking a bathroom break, rarely rested during breaks, and rushed to eat her lunch.

This also affected Peter's attitude toward God. Up until college, Peter's heart was filled with bitterness. "Why are you doing this to us?" he asked. "Do you really exist?" If God really existed, both his grandfather and father should have had better lives because they sacrificed everything for God. He didn't want to place his faith in such a God—a God who was irrational and unfair.

Because he thought logically and systematically, avoiding emotion, Peter majored in math and computer science. At that time, he believed more in evolution than creation. He thought evolution was based on scientific data.

But his mother prayed early every morning, placing her hands on Peter's and his siblings' heads; they felt her tears falling on them as they rested. Perhaps God heard her urgent prayers every morning for her children.

In his freshman year in college, my husband accepted Christ as his Savior. It happened when he attended a public debate between a UCLA professor who was an evolutionist and an MIT biology professor who believed in the creation theory. After the debate, Peter believed the theory of creation was actually more credible than evolution. This was God's grace and a miracle.

From that point on, my husband started to share the Gospel with other students on campus during his lunch breaks. From his witnessing, he saw many students come to Christ and found this miraculous.

He immediately went to his father and announced, "I want to be a missionary. I think it's my calling." He thought his father would be thrilled. Instead, his father responded, "Son, I'd like to see you become a person financially supporting the missionaries instead of becoming a missionary yourself."

■ ■

Perhaps his father responded this way because he didn't want the same hard life for his son. Nonetheless, my father-in-law emphasized the necessity of donors to support missionaries so the missionaries can focus on God's work.

Peter was then reminded of Ephesians 6:1, "Children, obey your parents in the Lord, for this is right." My father-in-law's advice brought brief disappointment to my husband, but this motivated him to make real plans to become a successful businessman in the future.

⌒

"What is your third question?"

I decided to urge him on with the next question. I watched his soft gaze and small smile and wondered what his intentions really were.

"So I have four siblings, but now that we're all grown up, it feels lonely. Five doesn't feel like a lot. So, when I get married, I'd like to have at least five children. What do you think about that?"

At that time in Korea, there was a national campaign to reduce the growth of the population. The government urged us with public slogans like "Two Children Only" or "One Child Only." It was a popular movement. For me, this question was unexpected since I had only thought about further pursuing my education. Also, I had not even thought about having children, let alone getting married. But I needed to respond. "Five children?" I laughed. "Well, if God gives them to me, I'll take them."

I wasn't completely sincere in my response. I thought he was joking, so I threw it back as a joke. But Peter was serious. He seemed to have taken what I said with total solemnity.

Our meeting was short, and it felt like I was being interviewed for an unknown job with three specific questions. I did not know at the time that these three questions would become the center and focus of my life.

When I came home, my mother asked, "How was it?"

"Well, it wasn't bad," I answered casually. I told her I didn't *dislike* him. I thought he was worth my consideration. But my mother responded with these weighty words, "If you don't dislike him, that's good enough for marriage."

The following day, his family expressed their wish to have the marriage take place. I panicked. I hadn't even graduated from college and suddenly felt rushed into a marriage for which I wasn't even ready. But my mother pushed me to marry, and I knew wholeheartedly that she lived her life one step at a time, one prayer at a time.

"*Sungjaya*, we want to see you marry this person. If you marry him and go to America, you could continue studying piano."

I recalled the words of my parents who refused to send me abroad to further my studies unless I married first. Also, this man's conviction was fresh on my mind. He wanted to live by faith and only for God's glory.

■ ■

I thought, *I might not be able to find somebody with that kind of faith, like this man's. If there is a soulmate somewhere out there for me, could he be the one?* As these thoughts crept up, my mother said, as if she read my mind, "*Sungjaya*, you know I have always prayed for your future husband. During one of my prayers, I saw his face. He had this man's face, the one you met yesterday."

Most parents won't lie to their children just to marry them off. And my mother was well known for her faithful prayers. She had spent most of her life praying and had on many occasions received answers to those prayers. So I did not believe she was lying.

My mother's firm belief that Peter was the one led me to marry him the following Thursday. Even though I had met him on the previous Wednesday, I felt peace in spite of the rush. I believed my parents prayed for me, day and night, from the minute I was born up to that moment. I used this assurance to find peace in my heart.

Our marriage took place within a week. Within a few months, I was in America.

Life in America proved challenging for me. I didn't speak enough English, so I couldn't leave the house by myself. And the period of adjustment living with my in-laws for a year was not easy. From early in the morning to late at night, my in-laws were either working or providing ministry to the church members. I felt helpless watching them work so hard.

"I am leaving for work now, so make the spinach salad." Every morning, my mother-in-law would order me to make

◼ ◼

side dishes for the family, in preparation for dinner. As she left, I would follow her out and wish her well. But I'd come back in, panicking, not knowing how to make any of these side dishes. I had never worked in a kitchen nor learned to cook growing up. Getting married didn't instantly give me the ability to make these dishes. The numerous mistakes I made in the kitchen and around the house completely dominated my life.

I also spent little time with my husband. We didn't date before getting married, and after we started living together in America, we didn't have time to discuss each other's day-to-day life and hardships. He was busy working during the day and studying business management at night. We also faced a major culture clash. My mind was strictly Korean while my husband's was more American. This clash added fuel to my burning loneliness in a foreign country.

My husband grew up in America; he was very certain about "yes" or "no," whereas we Koreans have a tendency to withhold our inner feelings. For example, one day after dinner with Peter, he asked me whether I would like to have an ice cream. In my Korean polite manner, I replied, "No, it's okay," even though I really wanted to have an ice cream. To be truthful, I was simply being polite by saying no, but he took my words literally. He stopped the car at an ice cream parlor, walked into the store, and bought an ice cream only for himself. Peter then got into the car and ate his ice cream without offering me a taste. *How could he do this to his wife?* I was hurt. And I wondered whether or not Peter actually loved me. Tears flowed frequently in our early stages of marriage. But it was only until later that I realized that the incident was entirely attributed to our cultural differences.

When I thought I couldn't bear the loneliness any longer, I heard these words from my doctor, "Congratulations. You're pregnant."

Being pregnant under these circumstances made my heart flutter with joy. Words cannot describe how I felt when hearing this news. To have a new life growing within me, when I was feeling so empty inside, filled my heart with joy and hope. As I prayed for my unborn baby, I felt blessed. *This child is clearly God's special gift*, I thought. In fact, when I was pregnant with Joseph, Pastor Park Kyung-Nam, who had arranged my marriage, briefly visited LA. I rushed to the airport to greet him as I was so glad to see him. When he saw that I was pregnant, he placed his hand on my unborn child and prayed that my baby would be a servant of God. After that prayer, Peter and I made the decision to dedicate Joseph to God as a missionary.

I thought of my husband's grandfather, who was not afraid to lose his life for God. I thought of my husband's parents, who set aside their personal ambition to follow God's calling. And then I thought of my husband, who ran around day and night, striving to be someone who supported missionaries. As these thoughts entered my mind, I knew God wanted to bless this family with good things.

I believed that God was sending the next generation to

this family to carry on God's grace, spread God's love, wash away our tears, and comfort us. These thoughts kept me happy during the full nine months of my pregnancy. That's why I overflowed with laughter when I heard our first baby crying in the delivery room.

This child is clearly God's special gift.

2

My Weak Fingers

Observing Korean-American customs, we gave our son two names, *Hong Yul* in Korean and Joseph in English. We named him Joseph because in Hebrew it meant "to add or increase," which was appropriate as he was our first "fruit." We also hoped our baby would grow up like Joseph in the Bible, who left for Egypt ahead of his brothers and solved the famine crisis for the Israelites.

I loved his thick eyebrows and his sweet, innocent smile. At times, when our eyes met, I was overwhelmed with happiness. I would often hold him close and rub my face against his. He was a part of me, but greater than me. I marveled at him as if he were something that had fallen from heaven, rather than come out of my body. I adored him.

Unfortunately, child-rearing involved a lot more than just wonder and amazement. Raising a child, especially my first

■ ▫ ■

child, was far more challenging than adjusting to a new language and culture of a foreign country. Not only was it difficult to put him to sleep at night, I also struggled to teach him new things. Joseph seemed more active than other babies his age. My husband's parents told me not to worry about Joseph's hyperactivity. They said, "He's just like his father. When Peter was little, he was overactive as well."

A new mom is like an explorer embarking on a new adventure; she sometimes gets lost in order to discover a new path. Nevertheless, it is every mother's mission to somehow get to a destination. As a novice in this journey of motherhood, I tended to turn right when someone said turn right and turn left when others said left.

I wished motherhood could be more like a new subject in school. I was frustrated and anxious at the fact that though I was pouring much more effort into motherhood than any academic work I had done before, it still seemed like I wasn't making any progress. As a student, if you worked hard, you could master any skill or knowledge. But raising a child? It seemed like I wasn't mastering anything at all no matter how hard I tried.

Ten months after Joseph was born, he was healthy. His eye contact was good, and so was his physical health. He was even taller and weighed more than average.

On a normal day mixed with joy and fatigue, I took Joseph to the hospital for his scheduled vaccinations at ten months. On my way to the hospital, I had no idea these steps would lead to the most life-changing moment of my son's life.

It happened such a long time ago that I don't remember

what the vaccines were for. Since it was a part of a routine immunization schedule, I can only guess it was either for diphtheria or the flu.

The accident came without any warning. When I carried Joseph to the doctor, he gave the vaccination with a dull facial expression.

Joseph screamed at the sharpness of the needle. I held him in my arms and comforted him.

"Joseph, did it hurt? It's all right. It'll be all right." I said. That's when the nurse discovered something wrong. She ran over to the doctor to inform him.

"What?" The shocked look on the doctor's face will forever remain vivid in my memory. He still seemed shocked for the next few minutes as he fidgeted and paced back and forth. He and the nurse continued to speak in hushed voices right in front of me. Back then my English wasn't good enough to understand their conversation. I barely understood how serious the situation was. All I heard intermittently were words like "ten months," "twenty-four months," and "overdosage." *Are they taking advantage of my weak grasp of the English language?* I wondered.

When their discussion finally ended, the doctor, who was now completely calm, called me back to explain the situation. He told me that although he accidentally gave Joseph an overdose, it shouldn't be a problem. The worst I would see was a fever, which could be remedied by aspirin or ibuprofen.

It turned out the doctor actually gave my ten-month-old Joseph the vaccine meant for a twenty-four-month-old baby.

■ □ ■ □ ■ □ ■ □ ■ □ ■ □ ■ □ ■ □ ■ □ ■ □ ■ □ ■ □ ■ □ ■ □ ■ □ ■ □ ■

Joseph, completely helpless and unaware, had been injected with an excessive amount of medicine.

Until that point in my life, I had never heard of immunization side effects. So, despite my suspicion and worry, I returned home trusting the doctor's words. At night, Joseph's fever was abnormally high. In those days, Koreans kept a type of medicine in the house called "*gheehung whan*," which is what I gave Joseph to temper his fever. I tried to console Joseph, but every "It's all right; it'll be all right" I repeated was really to console myself.

Diligently, I applied a cold cloth to his little body every night. Despite all I tried, Joseph's temperature would not go down, so I took him to a local hospital for a second opinion on his stubborn fever. Upon hearing that Joseph had received the wrong vaccine dosage, the emergency doctor phoned Joseph's doctor. However, the doctor who gave the excessive vaccination was suddenly unavailable.

When a baby is as young as ten months old, he hasn't fully developed an immune system. As a new mother, I had no idea how dangerous a higher-than-necessary vaccine dosage could be. All I wanted was for his temperature to go down as soon as possible. I believed that if his temperature just went down, all his problems would be solved.

The following day, I went to see Joseph's first doctor to get help for his fever. I had no idea this fever was just the beginning. My visit to the hospital proved to be in vain, because the doctor had resigned from the hospital.

Once I heard of his resignation, I felt as though black

clouds had penetrated my body. I thought, *Maybe I should find out where he lives and ask him about everything.* But there was no way for me to know if there was a connection between his resignation and Joseph's vaccination overdose.

Besides, as his mother, my first and foremost duty was to look after Joseph. I had to change his diapers, breastfeed him, put him to sleep, and give him medication. After several days, I didn't have the time to look for another doctor. In the meantime, Joseph's fever seemed to be getting milder. Therefore, I thought he was close to a full recovery.

At this point, however, Joseph's growth and development slowed down rather considerably. I couldn't erase the idea that the vaccine administration error might have inflicted critical damage to Joseph's brain.

When I suggested the vaccine error could be what caused Joseph's developmental disorder, most people, especially specialists, were rather critical and skeptical. They repeatedly told me there was nothing unusual about my child having a fever growing up. If a fever damages the brain, then every child would have a disability.

Multiple studies today confirm that vaccinations cannot cause autism.

Despite this, I could not shake the belief that an *overdose* of the vaccination had some detrimental effect.

Several years ago, a doctor at St. Joseph Medical Center in Bellingham, Washington, ran a test on Joseph to determine whether his autism was hereditary. The test results only confirmed my conviction that Joseph's disability was acquired after birth. But to this day, I have no idea what was actually in the vaccine my son received.

What is clear, though, is that Joseph had received an overdose long before there was any controversy around vaccinations. He was just a helpless ten-month-old baby whose only way of self-expression was crying and laughing. Without a choice of resistance, he received an overdose of chemicals that his small body couldn't handle. Other than the fact that his physical and mental development seemed slower, there weren't any other noticeable symptoms.

As days went on, putting him to sleep became more strenuous; he was physically too active and easily distracted. I thought maybe he had difficulties in comprehension because he was learning to speak in a bilingual environment. On top of that, I had just given birth to my second child, Samuel (or *Hong-Min*). Taking care of two sons, only a year and a half apart, was more than a handful. I soon became so busy that I even forgot about the overdose incident. I didn't even consider Joseph's slow development a major problem anymore, and my attitude was no different when Joseph turned three.

Because I couldn't handle Joseph while also caring for Samuel, I registered him at a half-day daycare.

One day, one of the teachers took me aside. "I find Joseph a bit strange."

I was confused. "Did you say 'strange'? What do you mean?"

I told her it was probably because his English wasn't fluent. When I got home, I thought about the conversation I had

■ ■

with the teacher and grew more offended. *Did it have something to do with him being Korean?*

In those days, racism against Asians was a reality. Thinking this could be the problem, I moved him to another preschool.

To my great disappointment, I heard the same comment at another school: "There is something odd about Joseph."

The new teacher's comment agitated, confused, and angered me. I thought maybe the teachers just weren't used to his hyperactivity.

Eventually, I looked for a preschool run by Koreans and decided to send him there. Even though the school was farther away from where we lived, we knew there would be no racial discrimination. As Joseph and I entered the new school hand in hand, I felt a sense of relief.

"Mrs. Chung, I'm afraid there may be something different about Joseph. Why don't you take him to a psychiatrist?"

My heart sank. I almost wished this comment was discriminatory rather than so ominous. *Does this mean he has a real problem?*

I immediately searched for a psychiatrist in LA and finally got an explanation.

"Your child is potentially autistic."

It was 1984. At that time, autism was not well known to the general public. I didn't have a clue what kind of illness it was.

I had no words. In ignorance, I simply thought if it were an illness, it could be treated immediately.

"Will brain surgery remove it?"

I was bewildered when the doctor told me there was no surgery for it.

"Then what do we do?"

"Right now there is no way to treat him."

I found the doctor's words preposterous. I didn't think any disease couldn't be healed. *Why has my son developed this disease in the first place? How is it possible that there are still incurable diseases?* Questions raced through my mind.

The doctor offered a solution. "Find a good teacher. A child like yours needs a good teacher. Medicine and operations won't help, but a good education will."

The doctor's suggestion left me feeling helpless. *How am I supposed to find a good teacher in this foreign country? And especially one who speaks Korean? Despite the education he gets, he may be ridiculed all his life. He may turn twenty and not be able to live by himself, let alone with a partner. How will he ever get married? I will always have to look after him. What will happen to him after I die?*

My heart tightened; my fears suffocated me.

I ran to God with this impossible problem. *God who made me, God who made Joseph. Oh God! Aren't you the Creator? God who made me, God who made Joseph. Why did you make Joseph like this and send him to me?*

I had never thought about Joseph like this before. To me, Joseph's face had shone brighter than any precious jewel. Now I saw a dark cloud above his face.

This change in perception was too painful. Joseph was

like the thumb of my hand. He was the healthiest and most handsome child; but once I found out he wasn't well, the pain gradually spread like a poison to the rest of my fingers. Then it spread to my whole body.

I tried to fix my thumb. I would touch it to see if it were functional, but the more I touched it, the more painful it became. Eventually I found myself not wanting to look at my thumb at all.

Around this time, my mother had come to America to help during my postpartum period. Once she learned about Joseph's condition, it broke her heart to see me hitting the lowest point of my life. Seeing that my two children were too much for me to handle alone and knowing I wasn't used to experiencing this kind of hardship, she decided to stay longer than planned to help me through the pain.

Carrying Joseph on her back, she would walk around our garden more than ten times a day singing Psalm Twenty-Three:

While the Lord is my Shepherd
I'm kept in His care,
like a lamb, dear and precious in His sight,
By the soft, flowing waters and the grass growing there
I find pasture and shelter day and night.
Yes, the Lord is my good Shepherd
I the lamb within His care!
He still leads me and feeds me where the green pastures
    grow,
and I lack nothing, ever anywhere!*

---

* *New Korean Hymn Book*, 570.

▫ ▫

The songs my mother used to sing to Joseph in the garden were not familiar tunes. They were neither modern gospel songs nor popular children's songs. They were desperate calls for hope and restoration from our forefathers born in the midst of war and devastation. These songs were about how greatly they needed God. These very songs became Joseph's lullabies.

> I hear Thy welcome voice
> that calls me, Lord, to thee
> For cleansing in Thy precious blood
> that flowed on Calvary,
> I am coming, Lord.
> Coming now to Thee:
> Wash me, cleanse me, in the blood
> That flowed on Calvary.*

She used to sing the fourth or fifth verses to Joseph in Korean, a language still completely foreign to someone struggling to communicate in even one language. Nevertheless, she would keep singing while walking around the garden ten or twenty times until Joseph fell soundly asleep strapped to her back. She sometimes sang fifty to a hundred different songs. Her peaceful singing was the only thing that allowed Joseph to sleep soundly every night.

One song I loved to hear went like this: "God is so good. God is so good. God is so good. He is good to me."

When I heard her singing, I couldn't help but cry, not

---

* *New Korean Hymn Book*, 254.

■ ■

because I was inspired emotionally or touched spiritually. I cried because I couldn't understand how she could praise God under these circumstances. I felt totally empty. I tried to find any trace of good in my life—to sing for joy—but I couldn't. I was moving further away from my days of youth when I never tired of playing the piano to praise God.

My mother continued singing her praises, "God is so good, God is so good …" I longed to feel whatever motivated her to sing a thousand times over to baby Joseph.

～

Every day was a battle. Once Joseph was diagnosed with autism, his characteristics became more noticeable to me. He often walked down the street and would suddenly hit any child he ran into for no reason. Eating and potty training were incredibly difficult for him. I couldn't take him to a playground or a restaurant.

There was no one for me to share the troubles my child and I were going through. I didn't even know where to begin and was afraid no one would be sympathetic to my situation. I had no one to confide in—no neighbors, no friends. Eventually, the number of days I spent inside to hide Joseph increased.

That didn't mean I felt more comfortable at home. Joseph was restless. Since he could go around the house and break things at any moment, I had to keep my eyes on him constantly.

Putting him to sleep, regardless of whether it was day or night, constantly challenged me. If I needed to put Joseph and two-year-old Samuel to sleep, I would take them for a drive. For some reason, Joseph was always fond of being in the car. He would stay calm and focus on whatever whisked by outside the window. After learning this secret, I drove day and night, until Joseph grew tired enough to fall asleep. Then I came home and put them both to bed. Sometimes, either Joseph or Samuel would wake up, and in the process, wake the other sleeping brother. So we'd pile back into the car for another drive. Frustrated tears streamed down my cheeks as I drove.

I drove around town endlessly to the point the mileage on my car for a single year equaled the average car owner's mileage for a lifetime. Around nine or ten at night, when my husband (who was working and going to school to earn an MBA) came home, my day finally ended.

In hindsight, I have great respect for my husband's diligent pursuit of purpose and vision throughout these challenging days. Back then, however, I resented him for his fixation on work. His time away amplified my loneliness.

At midnight I would go to bed with a sigh of relief. But when I awoke the next morning, desperation returned: *How am I to survive another day?*

I felt helpless. Even though my days would pass quickly, I longed for them to pass faster. I thought if I got older faster, I would see a quicker end to this painful life. I was living in a cave. Alone. Although my husband did his best for the family and my mother helped me throughout the day, I couldn't shake my growing feeling of loneliness. I couldn't even believe God was with me. Day by day, my body and mind deteriorated slowly. Days continued to feel like an endless race, a race where I was always alone.

Then one day, God couldn't leave me alone any longer. He sent me an angel.

A female pastor came to preach at Wilshire Korean Presbyterian Church, my father-in-law's church. They said she had a gift of prophecy. *Gift of prophecy? Is she a fortuneteller? Why do Christians need prophecy anyway?* I didn't understand.

Only later did I learn that the gift of prophecy was a spiritual gift from God, like the gift of speaking in tongues. Not meant to foresee the future, it was meant to comfort and encourage Christians in the present.

At that time, I was becoming skeptical of God's work altogether. I was still living only because I wasn't dead. I didn't even have faith to ask God for anything because I didn't believe he would answer. Having faith would mean living with God; but the only thing I was living with was my loneliness.

My mother-in-law told me to invite the pastor to our home for dinner. As soon as the dinner was over, the pastor asked me if she could pray for me. Her suggestion seemed a little sudden since she had no idea what I was going through. "Yes, you can pray for me." I just said yes. I had no expectation.

As I reluctantly went upstairs with her, I imagined this would be the same as every other time someone prayed for me. However, when we sat together to pray, I realized her words of prayer were on a completely different level. She wasn't praying to request something from God. Rather she relayed a message God had for me.

□ □

"Stephanie, you are not alone. God knows your pain and agony. He has been watching you all this time. What you are going through is all in God's plan." This was how the prayer began. I had not told anyone about my loneliness, so once I heard the word "alone," I couldn't control my tears. As if I had previously told this pastor about my daily life in great detail, she mentioned the specific conflicts within my family arising from my son's autism. She pinpointed my pains. She told me that God was fully aware of all my circumstances and that He wanted to help me as my Father. It was as if God diagnosed me through this pastor's prayer: "I know all your brokenness and pain. I know all your scars. I understand you."

God made it crystal clear that he knew my every cry. These simple words gave me unbelievable peace. I felt as if a gigantic wall had been knocked down in my heart. I no longer felt impeded. I was overwhelmed by waves of peace, which made me just cry and cry. I realized that my God had never left me; he had been walking with me, bearing all my burdens.

I experienced a small miracle through this prayer. Ever since I learned about Joseph's autism, a sickness had grown in my heart, and I had isolated myself by building walls. But that day, God healed me. Tears of joy washed all my pain away.

For the first time in my life, I realized God was never far away; he was with me everywhere, in every moment. While I was thanking God with joyful tears, the evangelist poured out blessings for me. She gave me God's promise in her prayer: "God allowed this suffering for you. If you endure it, you will see a green pasture and beautiful meadows stretched out before you. You will experience God's abundant blessings."

There was no doubt God sent his angel to me at the right time. After I realized God knew my suffering, I found strength to lift my weak fingers and touch the keys of a piano again. I finally opened my mouth to praise the Lord. I finally opened my eyes to see the small flame of my faith that I thought had been extinguished.

3

With Newly Awakened Eyes

The worst of his early childhood finally over, Joseph was now old enough to enter elementary school. However, there was no sign of real progress in his development, particularly in language acquisition, which is one of the recognizable signs of child development.

My husband and I tried to speak only English to avoid confusing him. Today a good amount of research has proven that autistic individuals can learn and speak several languages. However, back in those days, most were convinced creating a single-language environment would prevent confusion.

Despite our enormous efforts to converse with Joseph in English, all communication was frustrating. Even something simple, like calling his name, wouldn't elicit a response. Joseph still couldn't verbally express what he wanted. His behavior was so unpredictable that I couldn't even sit down and relax when I took him to a neighbor's house.

He also used to clog our toilets by stuffing all kinds of things into them. At first, I called in professional plumbers to fix the problem. After multiple house calls, we decided to buy a special tool to fix the problem ourselves. I unclogged that toilet so many times I could've become a professional plumber!

All I could think was: *Is he actually progressing?* Watching Joseph eat dinner quietly—after he had caused damage to our home—made me seriously question his growth and development. Agony crept in when I looked at Joseph. A fog would form around my head and would not go away.

Oh God, I understand that you want to train us so we will fulfill our mission on earth. We may be all right that way. But what about Joseph? What about his life? Isn't it too cruel for him?

I couldn't find answers to these questions. Joseph seemed to live in a labyrinth of pure chaos. *Would God really have a special plan for him?*

I tried to help him by searching for the best foods and nutritional supplements that were supposed to "help" Joseph. But nothing triggered any change in him.

I had to send him to school despite his special condition. No, in fact, I had to send him to school *because* of his condition. The doctor had said that a good education could be the only remedy to his autism.

Around this time, I heard about a unique public school

in the suburbs of LA that had a special education class taught by Marsha Tate, a teacher who specialized in children with autism. Although I still worried about Joseph having trouble with discrimination from non-Asian teenagers, I met Marsha and instantly her positive mind and clear philosophy on education dispelled my fear. Miss Tate assured me that even a child like mine could improve with the right education. "I am going to test your son with the alphabet."

I was taken aback when she said she was going to have Joseph write down alphabet letters as she read them out loud. How is that even possible? *There is no way*, I thought.

She smiled. "Do you think it is impossible? Well, all parents think that way in the beginning. Give me time, and you will see for yourself that Joseph will be able to write, read books, and do basic math, like addition, subtraction, multiplication, and division."

I could not believe what she was telling me. Even the most basic conversation had been difficult for Joseph. *How would he learn to read, write, and calculate when he could barely communicate with me?* I could not have predicted the dramatic growth in Joseph's life that took place in the six years that followed.

When Joseph began to receive specialized education from Miss Tate, he started to show exceptional abilities. First among them was his excellent memory. As he learned new vocabulary, Joseph always got 100 percent on his weekly spelling tests. He became so interested in words that he would carry a word search puzzle book with him all the time and complete a page a day. Despite his weakness in spoken words, Joseph was proving his strength in written words. He had beautiful penmanship. As he learned to write, Joseph made sure he paid attention to every single letter; his meticulousness was so extreme that people were always impressed by his artistic cursive handwriting.

Miss Marsha Tate helped us discover Joseph's small but special abilities. We became hopeful that Joseph could learn and do more. However, Joseph's school life was far from perfect. While we found glimmers of hope, we also faced darkness.

Holding on to this faith, I continued to serve as a church pianist. During worship and praise, I could lay down the heavy burdens of reality and feel free and light as if I were walking on a cloud.

"He hideth my soul in the cleft of the rock that shadows a dry, thirsty land; He hideth my life in the depths of His love, and covers me there with His hand." As I sang this hymn, I found my body and soul so comforted, if only until the end of the song.

Of course, my walk in the clouds never lasted long. As soon as the worship service ended, I staggered on the dusty, rugged road again. But the fact that I could walk with God through the music was enough to carry on—like finding an oasis in the middle of a desert.

Around this time, I learned that if we opened our reluctant mouths to praise the Lord, even during our suffering, our downtrodden souls could be revived.

My husband was always very busy with his studies and business. However, he always attended church to make it possible for me to play the piano. He also took care of the children during choir rehearsals to make sure that I could be there. Peter eventually bought an RV for Sundays. He would park the RV in the church parking lot and watch our five children, including Joseph. This allowed me to have a whole day at church without worrying about Joseph.

Peter wanted me to continue studying piano after I had our five children (Joseph, Samuel, Hannah, Esther, and Christian). Thanks to his support, I was able to continue despite my daily battles.

By God's grace, even when I floundered in the darkness, I could spread my ten fingers and praise him. There were days when my fingers ached; nevertheless, these fingers belonged to God, and he guided them to dance on the black and white keys of the piano.

While I was tied up looking after Joseph, my husband's business expanded day by day. He was fully living out the commitment he had made to me the first day we met to become a successful businessman to send out missionaries. Our family was even able to move to a house in Malibu.

The view around our new house was spectacular. This new place also perfectly fit our five children. However, my intensely busy days as a mother of five, especially with

Joseph's unpredictable behavior, kept me from appreciating the beautiful view.

As my husband's business grew, he frequently held big and small meetings at our place. Since we owned a beautiful house by the beach, we also opened our home to Peter's friends, who would use it for fundraising parties, weddings, and even as a filming location. Whenever such events took place, I always worried that Joseph would cause trouble and that people wouldn't understand him. These worries kept me from openly introducing him in public. Taking him out to other gatherings became almost unthinkable. Whenever I was to attend important meetings with Peter, I would hire someone to look after him. When Joseph's condition wasn't good enough for me to leave him, I would hide inside the house with him.

This happened on the day of King Coffman's wedding. King Coffman, who used to be the commander-in-chief of the 8th Army in Korea, was our longtime close friend. We offered our house for his wedding, and as the hostess, I had to pay close attention to every detail.

No matter the magnitude of the event, my thoughts were with my nine-year-old boy, Joseph. On this day, he was participating in a summer camp for special education students.

Joseph loved playing in water. Ever since he had learned how to swim, he never wanted to leave a pool. Picturing Joseph, who would be swimming in the ocean at camp that day, made me smile. Imagining him happily splashing in the waves erased any worries from my mind.

During the wedding event, the phone rang. The phone call was from Santa Monica Hospital. The woman on the phone said, "A boy by the name of Joseph has drowned!"

I couldn't understand what I was hearing. Joseph was such a good swimmer. How could he have drowned?

"Wait, did you say Joseph has drowned?"

"Yes. Surfers discovered him in the ocean, unconscious. They carried him out of the water, and he is in the hospital now."

Oh, God! When I heard this, I panicked. Being discovered by surfers meant he was swept way off from the shore.

I asked the dreaded question, "Is he dead or alive?"

The person on the other end wouldn't answer.

"Can you drive? Please drive safely." Those were the last words I heard before the line went dead.

I dropped the telephone and ran to the car mumbling, "Joseph. It can't be Joseph. Joseph. You can't die!"

Upon hearing the news, I almost lost my mind. I even forgot the fact that I was hosting a wedding. Later, I learned that when the guests saw me running, they immediately thought something had happened to Joseph and started to pray for him.

As soon as I got into my car, I sped toward the hospital.

Joseph, I'm coming. Just hold on.

Like a chant, I repeated to myself, "Don't die. You can't die." On my way to the hospital, Joseph's life started to flash before my eyes. I saw Joseph, who came into my life as a melody and was later pierced by people's thorny eyes. Joseph had suffered his whole life. It tore my heart.

■ □

Oh God, what kind of sinner am I?

Seeing the snapshots of Joseph's life filled me with agony. I moaned. I sighed.

Oh, Lord, what have I done? I am a sinner.

I prayed, *Father God, I am a sinner among sinners. There is nothing good in me. I complained about Joseph. I was blind and could not see how you tried to show your perfect love though Joseph. I did not know how to love Joseph as a mother. I said I loved him with words, but I was always angry with him in my heart. I even thought about harming him. I am a sinful, stupid mother.*

I remembered the moment I contemplated taking my life and his. It wasn't long after Joseph had been diagnosed with autism. I was at the hospital with Joseph. I looked down the window of the towering hospital, and a suicidal thought attacked my mind. I wanted to jump with Joseph. It was only a momentary impulse, but looking back, how dare I think I could end his life.

I had to ask forgiveness from the God who created Joseph and who had been leading his life.

Oh, God, I treated Joseph as though he were dead. While he wanted to play outside, I confined him to a room. I did not have the eyes to see the value of my son, whom you have loved and sent with a purpose. I treated him as one who only bothers his siblings and causes nuisance to other people. I often thought, "What are you going to do with your life, Joseph? You wouldn't even be good at anything." Lord, you embraced me—a wretched sinner—as I am. But I did not accept him as he was. Please forgive me, Lord.

■ □ ■ □ ■ □ ■ □ ■ □ ■ □ ■ □ ■ □ ■ □ ■ □ ■ □ ■ □ ■ □ ■ □ ■ □ ■ □ ■ □

On the way to the hospital, I shed a flood of tears and was overwhelmed by the heavy burden that suppressed me. I was coming to the realization of how serious my sins were. I felt like I would die from the pressure.

Father, forgive my sins. I cannot bear the weight. Save me, Lord. Please wash me clean. I can only be saved by the blood of Jesus. Jesus, you alone can rescue me. Lord, forgive my sins. Remove the burden of my sins!

And finally, at the end of the prayer, I confessed, *Lord, please let Joseph live. I will never ask for more. You do not have to heal his autism. I will be happy and ever grateful for who he is. So please let him live. He is perfect as he is.*

To get to the hospital, the drive usually took fifteen minutes. That day, it felt like it took well over an hour because thoughts and emotions flooded my mind. When I reached the emergency room, I found Joseph. His belly was swollen, having ingested too much water. He looked like a pregnant woman. Seven or eight doctors stood around him.

Doctors and nurses moved quickly about, from afternoon to night. They were doing their best to pump the water out of his stomach. The color of the water being emptied made me ever more nervous. Due to various impurities from the sea, it was dark purple.

The ER doctors did all they could. Finally, they moved Joseph to a room. Upon leaving, one of the doctors spoke to me, "He is still in a coma. If he does not wake up in the next forty-eight hours, I am afraid he will die or be paralyzed."

What? The words barely registered. It couldn't be!

The doctor told me to prepare for the worst-case scenario. When he left the room, I took Joseph's limp hand in my shaky one and pleaded to God for him to wake up.

Until that moment, I had rarely prayed so earnestly. Not knowing if Joseph would survive till morning, I prayed and prayed until I felt like my heart was melting. I told the Lord I would be so happy if only I could walk hand and hand with Joseph again, if only I could rub his face until it warmed, and if only I could see his innocent eyes once more. I told him I would love Joseph the way God has loved me, if he would just let Joseph live. I told God there would be no greater grace if I could be given another chance to love him. I was making a genuine confession that Joseph was more precious to me than anything else in the world.

I must have prayed for several hours and fallen asleep. I awoke early the next morning, not sure if God had answered my prayers. The doctors and nurses still doubted whether Joseph would recover. Had my son made it through the night? In half doubt, I softly called his name.

I did not hear anything in return. Joseph was not a particularly responsive boy, so his lack of response could've been normal, but I still wasn't sure …

Was my son alive?

To check, I put a straw in a cup of water and gently brought it to his lips. "Joseph, try to have a sip." At that very moment, Joseph sipped with his eyes still closed.

He was alive! Even though Joseph hadn't yet opened his eyes, I felt as if my heart would explode.

When I poured another cup of water on the small table next to his bed, Joseph turned his head toward me and gulped down the water.

Thank you, Lord! My heart overflowed with gratitude. *You answered my prayers!*

I called the nurses outside to let them know Joseph had woken up. The doctors and nurses were overjoyed at the sight of Joseph miraculously awake after many hours. Joseph looked at everyone with the same innocent eyes as ever.

After again pouring my gratitude out to God, I was relieved enough to think of our family waiting at home for news. I left Joseph with the doctor and hopped into my car. I gripped the steering wheel as tears flowed. *Oh, Lord*, I prayed. Joseph is alive! It is all by your grace! It is all by your love!

That night, Joseph had stood at the crossroads of life and death, and God had mightily saved him. He had been unconscious but now acted normal—as if he had just had a good night's sleep. I praised God all the way home. God's amazing grace was the only reason for Joseph's ability to drink water, to walk, and to enjoy his life!

I experienced something new and marvelous on the way home. Just overnight, the same road I had known for years suddenly appeared completely different.

I could not believe all the dazzling sights. As the sun rose over the horizon, each blossom basked in its warmth. The lush leaves danced in praise for the Lord. The birds stretched wings, soaring as if diving into the sky's infinite embrace. The ocean and its swaying waves left me speechless. Words weren't enough.

God's creation was magnificent.

For the first time in my life, I saw how truly beautiful the world really was.

How can the world be transformed overnight? Why couldn't I see all these wonderful things before? As I headed home, I experienced a whole new world. I felt as though I had been looking at the world through dark lenses, and now they had been removed.

My sight wasn't the only thing that changed. I no longer had to drag my feet as though burdened with a heavy load. In fact, my whole body felt as light as a feather—I thought I could fly like a bird. Even though I had hardly slept, I didn't feel tired at all.

I remembered the words to the hymn. "He hideth my soul in the cleft of the rock that shadows a dry, thirsty land; He hideth my life in the depths of His love, and covers me there with His hand." This was the story of my life.

My realization of sins and repentance, the rediscovery of God's love, along with Joseph's recovery, triggered an instant transformation. When morning came, I was given new eyes and a new body. I could not stop the joy and gratitude flowing out of me.

After Joseph woke up, I was finally in the right state of mind to thank the person who had rescued Joseph. I was told that a young man who was waiting to catch a wave far from the shore found Joseph's body which had been swept up. He had carried Joseph out of the water and had brought him back to Joseph's teacher. In the midst of the emergency, the camp instructor had not even asked the man his name. The police had arrived later at the scene to investigate and had not been able find the young man.

If the young man hadn't been there at that critical moment, Joseph would have died. Every now and then, whenever I pass the beach, I say a thanksgiving prayer to God for sending an angel that day. Although I do not know where he is or what he is doing, I pray that God may bless him and that many people may show him kindness.

Having been showered by God's mercy, we began to live a brand-new life. The day after the accident, my life turned from hell to heaven. Above all, I became genuinely thankful for Joseph just as he was; joy overflowed in my heart.

As a result of the accident, I really felt the heart of God. Once that love became tangible to me, love began to spring from my heart, and the kingdom of God was everywhere I looked.

As a parent, I was also transformed. There was a domino effect from me to the rest of my family. In fact, it would be more correct to say God's immeasurable love enveloped my entire family all at once. We all loved Joseph even more than before. To be exact, our eyes and hearts were opened to see how we should truly love Joseph.

From then on, no matter who visited our house, I would call Joseph out and proudly introduce him. I couldn't help doing it—Joseph was now so lovely to me that I wanted everyone to meet him. I would say, "This is Joseph, our eldest son. Joseph, say, hello to everyone."

◼ ◻ ◼

It had been the opposite before; I would stay and play in his room, never wanting to introduce him to our guests. But now I no longer felt embarrassed. Joseph was perfect in my eyes. He must have felt it too, because he suddenly became more cheerful.

"Hi, how are you? My name is Joseph. What is your name?"

Joseph's distinct way of greeting people began around this time. I finally learned that Joseph just wanted to greet people and be close to them. How could I have treated such a sociable and friendly boy the way I used to? How could I have hurt his self-esteem like that?

I had thought Joseph was incapable of knowing whether people liked or disliked him or whether they were proud or ashamed of him. But all along, he was fully aware of everyone. He was more sensitive than other people; he was even sensitive enough to notice the small changes within our family.

Around this time, Joseph's uncontrollable behavior began to calm down. Joseph, who used to be so restless and unsettled, started to practice writing letters of the alphabet quietly at his desk. Furthermore, his teachers began complimenting him.

His ability to use language to communicate with others improved little by little. The more he interacted with people, the more he became attentive to what they were saying. He finally began to express himself with just a word or two.

Joseph and Peter sang together. In the past, during family worship, Joseph would either sit like a rock or get up and wander around. Now, he proved to us that he remembered the lyrics of the hymns his grandmother used to sing to him.

◻ ◻

When I said, "Let's sing," he would sing all four verses in Korean from memory. One day, he surprised us even further. I suggested, "Why don't you pray for us today, Joseph?" Joseph closed his eyes and said the words of a prayer in the exact words that the family had prayed for him.

"Oh Lord, Father, heal me. Father Lord, help me get healed."

Joseph must have repeated the same phrase for two to three minutes. Finally, when he got to the end, he paused after saying, "Lord." Then he continued by saying "Jesus" and then emphasized every syllable.

"Heal me. I pray in the name of the Lord, JESUS. Amen!"

4

Hope in the Wilderness

After the accident, we started living completely renewed lives. Joseph allowed us see to see how he could improve every day.

But in time, Joseph had to go through puberty like everybody else, which came with a lot of confusion and hardship. Because Joseph struggled to control his emotions, the sudden ups and downs of his hormones had an enormous impact on him. This period exhausted both Joseph and us. We felt like the Israelites when they wandered into the wilderness after escaping Egypt.

Middle school was completely different from elementary school. Some students grew so rapidly you could barely distinguish students from teachers.

One day, when Joseph happened to go to the washroom alone, he was badly beaten. He was left to bleed until a student found him lying on the washroom floor. When teachers heard the report, they immediately transported him to the nearest emergency room where he received twelve stitches on the back of his head. When I was notified, I was in extreme shock and rushed to the hospital.

In desperation, I asked him, "Joseph! Who did this to you?! Joseph, tell Mom!"

No matter how many times I repeated the question, his answer only came in silence. I was angry for what had happened to my son. I hadn't been at the scene of the crime, but I could picture Joseph unable to fight back while being beaten for no reason. He couldn't have even uttered, "Stop it."

My heart shattered into a million pieces. As a desperate measure, the school authorities made some troublesome students stand before Joseph. The authorities asked Joseph to pick out which students hurt him. However, Joseph was unable to say anything. He was unable to even lift a finger. He seemed completely unaware how serious the situation was. Instead he looked casually around as if none of this mattered to him.

After some investigation, it was believed that to join a gang, a student had to knock out another person. One of the potential gang members chose Joseph as a target. This incident magnified my worry for Joseph. *How on the earth will Joseph survive and protect himself in this tough reality? He cannot even identify the person who hurt him.*

God only stood by, silent, no matter how much I prayed. The thought that I couldn't do anything for Joseph as a parent paralyzed me. All I could do was grit my teeth.

□ □

Does God really love us? If He does, why do these things happen to Joseph?

On one hand, I shook like a helpless tree amid a storm. Since learning about Joseph's disability, I always had to wrestle with my questions about God and pain. On the other hand, I remembered the Gospel I had heard from my Sunday school days. I clung to God's words and hung on to my feeble faith.

I kept repeating to myself, "God is love. God is good. He uses the weak to do things in a mighty way. Therefore, there must be a special purpose for Joseph too. Certainly, God would never leave Joseph as a victim of bullying."

During puberty, children have a hard time dealing with their emotions. Because of this, many parents become angry with them for their impulsive behavior. Sometimes, they think they must correct their children immediately by scolding and lecturing them. Fathers, especially, tend to judge their children solely on their behavior. They're quick to reprimand their children's bad behavior to prevent trouble later. Joseph's father was no different. Peter loved Joseph, but he was strict with him; he was worried Joseph would make other people uncomfortable.

However, when Peter disciplined him, Joseph became more and more anxious. His bursts of rage and compulsive behavior gradually worsened. The worst arguments of my married life happened in those days. My husband focused heavily on fixing Joseph's behavioral problems, and I insisted on giving him time and space.

At that time, there were very few studies on autistic children, and even the ones that existed were insufficient. There

■ ❑ ■ ❑ ■ ❑ ■ ❑ ■ ❑ ■ ❑ ■ ❑ ■ ❑ ■ ❑ ■ ❑ ■ ❑ ■ ❑ ■ ❑ ■ ❑ ■ ❑ ■ ❑ ■

was still no speech therapy or social therapy. No one actively discussed how parents should approach their children. It wasn't until much later that we came to understand the basic principles of parenting. Parents should be strict in disciplining their young children but exercise patience and acceptance during puberty.

All I could do in those days was to keep praying and asking God, "Lord, what should I do?"

In response, he spoke to me calmly in silence. He told me to have a gentle love that gives hope while also bearing and enduring all things. The most effective way to bring about change in people was patience and unconditional love. In reality, to practice patience meant extreme loneliness. During this time, whenever Joseph became angry, he ran outside because he couldn't control his rage. Sometimes he even grabbed and pulled my hair. This made me shudder, not because of the physical pain but because of the indescribable heartache I felt.

On one day, Joseph's impulsive behavior, which was more severe than usual, baffled me. Unable to control his temper, Joseph grabbed my hair, which made me fall to the marble floor. Suddenly, I was a mother who had just been thrown onto the floor by her own son. He had grabbed my hair so fiercely that he even held a handful in his hand. I felt severe pain in the back of my head; however, within a millisecond, the unbearable heartache that was much worse than the physical pain rushed in.

Should I go to the doctor? If I go to see the doctor, what would I even tell him?

Moreover, I did not know how to tell Peter, who already constantly worried about me with Joseph. I simply couldn't handle what Peter would do or say if he knew what had happened.

I was even reluctant to tell my closest Korean friend. Eventually, I called an American friend and went to the hospital. The fact that I couldn't even decide whom to call in this dire moment made me feel utterly alone.

Yet in the midst of the pain and worry, something made me happy. It seemed that Joseph felt real remorse toward me for the first time in his life. He couldn't control his anger because he didn't understand his actions had consequences. Yet, I could see him feeling sorry for what had happened. I was incredibly grateful for his sincere regret.

Looking at Joseph, who now had the ability to feel remorse, I found a reason to hope a little longer. Although his reckless behavior was still present, I had real hope that it might go away.

Romans 5:3–4 reads, "Not only so, but we also glory in our sufferings, because we know that suffering produces perseverance; perseverance, character; and character, hope." Through Joseph, I was learning the lessons of the living Word in my own life.

Years passed and I continued to have faith in God's message about suffering. Gradually, just as I had hoped, Joseph's brash behavior began to disappear. In fact, Joseph was growing into a wholesome young man.

I'm not saying these years of waiting were easy. But I have firsthand experience at seeing how a parent's faith in a child can bring about positive change. In a lot of ways, Joseph's period in the wilderness was a time of growth for me as well.

In raising Joseph, I learned that a child's mind is forever connected to his parents through an invisible umbilical cord. When parents become frustrated with their children, children can feel worthless. But if parents persistently believe in their children and believe that God will use them in a significant way, the challenge can be overcome. Joseph is proof of this victory.

I believe parents do not need to be anxious about their children's troublesome behavior. I forced myself to be more relaxed and patient toward my son, and I was able to even laugh about Joseph's behavior. I learned that children will never totally forsake their parents' patience.

⌣

Joseph had another problem, which began just before puberty. Because of this problem, which always manifested suddenly, we were in a constant state of emergency. Joseph's autism was concurrent with ADHD (attention deficit hyperactivity disorder). When he was seven, he started taking medication to alleviate his hyperactivity. But he felt the medicine's adverse effects almost immediately. Joseph not only lost his appetite, his lips turned blue, and he would become totally lethargic. I felt so bad for him that I had to discontinue his medicine. I thought it would be better to deal with his hyperactivity than to see him so lifeless.

Parents would hate to give medication to their children that had major side effects. I felt that way as well. However, a few years later, I was giving Joseph an even stronger medication that not only negatively impacted his liver but also had other complicated effects; it was an antiepileptic drug to suppress seizures. Joseph had his first epileptic attack when he was seven after he stopped taking his medication for ADHD, Ritalin. Desperate, I felt I had no other choice but to make him take the medication that suppressed his seizures.

Autism, although a difficult disability, is not fatal. Epileptic seizures, on the other hand, can kill people by blocking their air passage. Therefore, I was determined to find a cure for his epilepsy and took Joseph to countless doctors. But nothing seemed to help.

One of the biggest challenges for a parent of an autistic child is how physically demanding it is on the parent. The parent must hold her child's hand, speak for him when he cannot express his needs, play with him, and follow him everywhere. As a result, a mother of an autistic child lives with intense muscle pain and chronic weariness.

With Joseph's dual condition, although I still had the weight of the autism issues, I couldn't do anything physically for him. Whenever he had a seizure, all I could do was clench my pained heart and pray. As he grew taller and bigger, I couldn't stand to watch his fully grown adult body collapsing before my eyes. My powerlessness to help my son gave me agony beyond words.

Oh Lord, we can live with his autism, but please heal his epilepsy. Dear Jesus, please heal him.

Despite my incessant tears, prayers, and hope, Joseph's epilepsy did not improve. Finding the right medication was a constant struggle. And even if I found one that worked, it was only temporary; it merely reduced the frequency of seizures and suppressed the symptoms temporarily. Sometimes, I saw him completely fine during the day but suffering at night. During a good week, Joseph only had one seizure. The worst he ever had was seven or eight seizures in a single night. The morning after that ordeal, he was completely exhausted. However, his obsessive habit to follow his daily regiment forced him to get up at a certain time and push himself through the day. As a mother, my heart broke to see him struggle. All I wanted was for him to rest, but the only thing I could do for my beloved son was to watch him struggle through his routines.

I was determined to find a cure no matter what it took. For a long period of time, to find a cure and to get the right medication, the hospital became the place where we went together most often, besides school. Joseph was always prescribed the maximum dosage, most likely because his epilepsy was so severe. That's why he was required to have a blood test for his liver check every three months. I'm not sure whether it's the same for other illnesses, but in the case of Joseph, even if a drug seemed to work initially, it lost its effectiveness after a year or two. The seizures would always return.

Moreover, whenever he changed to a new medication, he had to endure a new set of side effects. At one point his weight even went as high as 220 pounds because of the adverse effects of the drugs. When he switched to a different medication, his

□ □

weight dropped as low as 150 pounds. Despite this, I still had him try various medications, hoping it would prevent multiple seizures.

In spite of frequent hospital visits and changes in medication, Joseph's epilepsy did not go away. During a seizure, he would fall with a yelp and have facial paralysis while his eyes rolled back. Only the whites in his eyes could be seen as he involuntarily drooled from the paralysis. Due to his severe jerking, any object could turn into a dangerous weapon. Therefore, when he started to have a seizure, my first priority was to remove the objects around him. Then I would give him a leg massage as I desperately called out to the Lord, *Oh Lord, help him. Wake him up. Lord, please help.*

On average, a short seizure would last about forty-five seconds. If longer, it lasted about a minute and forty-five seconds. However, to me, short or long, it felt like forever. During a seizure, the thought would cross my mind that Joseph might stop breathing. It felt as if my heart would stop too. When Joseph finally exhaled at the end of the seizure, I would stop shaking. After the cessation of the seizure, exhausted of all his energy, he would fall into a deep asleep. Then I would sink into the floor, burying my face into his chest, and wipe my tears.

Since I lived the same awful moment repeatedly, my husband, as a thoughtful gesture, suggested we take a family trip on a cruise. He wanted to give us a break from our daily battles.

But even with the beautiful backdrop of the ocean, Joseph still collapsed on the ship's deck. *Thud.* The noise startled the crowd, and I saw Joseph's body jerking. After this particularly violent seizure ended, it took him a while to calm down and fall asleep.

That night, as I wiped my tears, I stood alone on the deck and asked out loud, "Oh Lord, where are you?"

A flood of agony came over me. I doubted whether we would ever reach the land of Canaan at the end of this seemingly endless journey through the wilderness. It was a pitch-black night. When I looked around, the indigo blue ocean was the only thing that surrounded me. My knees shook with emptiness and fear. In that moment, a strong impulse to disappear into the dark ocean below came over me. I had lost the energy required to walk through this dry and weary land. Because of Joseph's near-drowning accident, I had never thought of ending my own life, no matter how hopeless I had felt. I was a wife and a mother of five—how could I have such an awful thought? However, that night, as though I was haunted, I could not think of anything else. The only thought ruling my mind was that if I were to jump into the ocean, my misery would be over. From the deck, all I had to do was lift a leg, fall into a black hole and end my suffering.

Death shows up in unexpected moments. It felt as though something pulled me, and all I wanted to do was let it pull me all the way in.

All of a sudden, as if someone had smacked the back of my head, my mind returned to reality. It occurred to me that if I stayed here any longer, I would do something absolutely terrible. I left quickly, running to escape death.

Lord, I'm being tempted by a demon. Lord, please hold me, help me. I repeated this prayer, trembling.

After this incident, any time my mind went to that dark place, I would open my mouth and praise God.

What matters where on earth we dwell?
On mountain top, or in the dell,
In cottage, or a mansion fair,
Where Jesus is, 'tis heaven there.[*]

Whenever I sang this hymn, it made me think, *Lord, whether Joseph has autism and epilepsy or not, as long as we are with you, everywhere is heaven.*

Joseph loved this hymn. Even when Joseph lay helpless after a seizure, I would remind myself of this song to give me peace.

---

[*] Charles F. Butler and James M. Black, "Where Jesus Is, 'Tis Heaven," 1898.

5

Praising God

We had to move twice during Joseph's wilderness stage. First, we went to Seattle. My husband's businesses, which had grown steadily, now fell one by one. We had no choice but to move. However, we firmly believed moving to Seattle was, by the grace of God, the foundation of our new start. We could serve and be loved while attending the Community Church of Seattle. This is where we rediscovered the true meaning of suffering. It was also the time for my husband to revisit his original calling of becoming a businessman. His success in business was all achieved by the grace of God. Peter repented of his pride and sought guidance in God's Word. For the next three to four years, he traveled around the world to discover new business opportunities. Finally, he was able to launch an education business.

Joseph was sixteen years old when we left for Vancouver,

Canada. We followed my husband's path after a long period of preparation. Since Joseph especially loved the ocean, we moved to a new house by White Rock Beach, near the US border. There, my family embarked on a new journey.

As soon as we moved from Seattle to Vancouver, we encountered a new problem. Even though we had moved, I didn't want to leave the church in Seattle because I was still serving as a church pianist at the time. After much discussion, we decided to keep attending the Community Church of Seattle.

However, we weren't sure if Joseph was able to make the long trip from Vancouver to Seattle every Sunday. It took over two hours each way. He still displayed impulsive behavior and lived by a strict schedule; therefore, I doubted whether it would be possible to wake him up earlier in the morning to leave for church. We couldn't leave him alone at home either, so we decided to try it out and make the final decision later.

The first trial Sunday, I woke the kids in the early morning to go to church. I put everyone in the car, including an extremely unhappy Joseph. Immediately after we crossed the border and passed Bellingham, I heard the kids scream from the back of the car. Joseph, who sat in the backseat, began to have a seizure.

My husband pulled over to the side of the road and promptly ran to help Joseph. When he saw Joseph, tears streamed down his face. Peter had never cried in front of the kids, but seeing Joseph suffer, he couldn't help but sob.

Oh Lord, when will Joseph's suffering stop?

■ ■

It took a while for Joseph to feel better. We went to church and attended service with broken hearts. Indeed, we all felt like bruised and sorrowful reeds.

After the incident, we realized that taking Joseph all the way to Seattle was too much for him. I had to think hard about what to do. We found a church called Canada Immanuel Church, which was within walking distance from where we lived. Fortunately, Joseph loved this church. Every Sunday, our family went to the Community Church of Seattle while Joseph stayed in Canada with his caregiver and attended Canada Immanuel Church.

One Sunday, I awoke early to prepare for service. That morning, my head hurt from trying to work out Joseph's schedule. Canada Immanuel Church had moved to a new location, and Joseph would not be able to attend Sunday service that day. Although it only took about twenty to thirty minutes by car, Joseph's caregiver did not drive.

Not having found a solution, I had to tell Joseph, "Joseph, you're not going to church today. The church has moved to a different place. Just for today, can you have Sunday service at home with your caregiver?"

I knew how much Joseph loved going to church on Sundays—more than anything. After hearing this bad news, he immediately became angry.

We said goodbye to Joseph and left for church. The only thing on my mind was finding a way for Joseph to go to church every Sunday—and the sooner the better.

We arrived in Seattle to attend the service. After the service and choir practice, I received a phone call from Joseph's caregiver. "Hello? There's a problem! Joseph is lost. Gone!"

"What? What do you mean?"

Joseph had to be home. I didn't understand how he could be lost in his own house. I took an extra breath and asked what happened. After all, I couldn't leave and search for him right away; it would still take hours to get home even if I left immediately.

The caregiver gave more details. "At about eleven o'clock, Joseph told me he wanted to go to church and insisted that he had to be at the eleven o'clock service. I explained to him that the church had moved, and we couldn't go today. Joseph became angry and dashed out of the house. I ran after him, but he disappeared."

Suddenly, everything went dark.

If he's not around the house, where else could he be? He could be lost and wandering around! I started desperately praying that Joseph would find his way back. I waited for another phone call, clutching my burning heart.

Later I found out that Joseph had run along the street, crossed several intersections, made a left turn, ran through the trees, and crossed another intersection. He ran and walked and ran and walked for a long time. He headed straight to Canada Immanuel Church, thinking about only one thing, to get there on time for the eleven o'clock service.

It takes at least three hours on foot to the new church location. Joseph had been there only twice with me—and by car. On that Sunday, he decided to run the distance.

■ ■

Surprisingly, after about three hours, Joseph made it to church. Rev. John Alan found Joseph trying to catch his breath in the front yard of the church. The service had already ended and Reverend Alan was just about to lock the door.

Later, he told me he was surprised to find Joseph standing outside the church. *Why is Joseph here at the church by himself?* he had wondered. *What would have happened if he had arrived just a minute later? No one would have been at the church!*

Rev. Alan gave Joseph a ride home. When I heard his story, I couldn't believe it. It was a complete mystery. I would not have been able to make it there had I tried to walk to the church. How did Joseph remember the route? And how did he manage to avoid the cars while crossing the streets? Even to this day, whenever I drive by the church, I give thanks to God for keeping Joseph safe that day.

Like other mothers raising children with disabilities, I believed Joseph had to be looked after every single minute. I constantly thought about what would happen after I died. *Who would take care of him?*

God watched over him for the three hours I wasn't there. When no one was looking after him, God protected even the hair on his head. The only possible conclusion we could draw was that God sent an angel to protect Joseph while the rest of the family had gone to worship the Lord.

That night, in addition to a prayer of thanks, I came to realize that my judgment about Joseph had been wrong. I pushed out the thoughts that had accumulated deep in my

◼ ◻ ◻ ◻ ◼ ◻ ◻ ◻ ◼ ◻ ◻ ◻ ◼ ◻ ◻ ◻ ◼ ◻ ◻ ◻ ◼ ◻ ◻ ◻ ◼ ◻ ◻ ◻ ◼ ◻ ◼

mind for a long time: *He doesn't understand the sermon any-way. It's not going to be much different if he stays behind and worships at home for one Sunday.*

These were my passing thoughts, but Joseph demonstrated his deepest desire that day by his actions as a wake-up call for his ignorant mother: he too wanted to go to church on Sundays to worship God. The very reason for his life was to praise God and to worship him.

~

"Will Joseph ever be able to have faith?"

During Joseph's childhood, I used to ask myself this question often. Faith is hard to grasp, even if we share the Gospel with people who have the cognitive ability to understand; it is difficult for them to believe in Jesus. So then, how could my child, who struggled to have a basic conversation, be able to believe in Jesus and walk with him? I was doubtful.

Despite my weakening faith, I had held Joseph's hand and prayed for him every night. His grandparents had sung hymns while piggy-backing him. And his family members had shared the Word of God during family services whether or not Joseph appeared to be listening.

All this time, I had never expected Joseph to have a faith of his own. I reasoned that he went to church because we took him there and that he listened to my prayer only because I prayed for him every night before bedtime.

Even after Joseph entered elementary school, I held this

understanding. No matter how I tried, I believed he could never be saved by personally accepting Jesus as his Savior and relying on him for salvation. We had all failed to understand the power of God's love to speak to every heart, including Joseph's.

In the meantime, Peter and I decided to send Joseph to a program called Respite Service, a program designed for parents of children with disabilities. The parents could get a well-deserved break by sending their children to a specially trained teacher for two to three days.

When Joseph's teacher introduced me to the program, my feelings were both hopeful and anxious. Children like Joseph tend to feel uneasy in unfamiliar environments. For example, even something as simple as different wallpaper can cause them to have difficulty falling asleep. Likewise, Joseph didn't do well if he didn't follow a certain routine. For that reason, Joseph's room was always tidy and in order.

How could a child like this fall asleep at night in a complete stranger's home? I worried that he might scream all night from anxiety, even be traumatized. That's why, as a parent, I was cautious to try anything new or different for Joseph.

I learned that exposing children to a new environment was not only essential for the parents, but also for the children. Parents should try this (to a certain extent) to help disabled children overcome the fear of a new environment. Children who have been exposed to different places demonstrate less stress when they confront inevitable changes in their later lives.

■ ■

Of course, at that time, I did not have this knowledge. All I could do then was pray for Joseph to survive two nights without causing any trouble in a new environment.

On my way to the teacher's house, I told him repeatedly, "Joseph, you are going to be sleeping there for two nights. You will sleep two nights in the teacher's house. You will have fun." Joseph didn't reply, but what would these words have meant to him anyway? Still I repeated this numerous times, wanting him to be able to understand even just a little bit.

When we finally got to the house, Joseph looked around the strange room, awkwardly. I suddenly became hesitant and unsure whether I could leave him. The teacher urged me to leave immediately to help Joseph adjust quickly. At this advice, I turned around to leave, but Joseph gripped my arm. Never had Joseph reached out to me first.

"We pray." Joseph asked me to pray for him. With his own mouth, he asked me to pray for him. Again, I was completely surprised. All this time, I thought Joseph considered prayer as only one of his nighttime routines, which we did before he went to bed, similar to his morning routine of awaking at eight, eating his breakfast, and brushing his teeth.

But it wasn't nighttime, and yet he was still asking me to pray. I was deeply touched that he recognized the new situation. Furthermore, he was trying to overcome his anxiety with the power of prayer.

Immediately I told him, "Yes, Joseph. Let's pray. I will pray for you." I held his hands tightly and prayed that God would protect him for the two nights and that he would be comfortable there. Joseph confidently replied, "Amen!" When the prayer ended, Joseph smiled and gestured that I could go home now. This incident made me think about faith in a whole new way.

I wondered: What is faith? Or rather, in which category does faith belong?

Faith or having faith in God belongs not in the realm of intellect and reasoning. It belongs to a whole new dimension of spirituality. If a person is highly intelligent, he or she may not be spiritual. On the other hand, if a person lacks intelligence, we can never say he or she is less spiritual. This is the reason why, when it comes to experiencing God and living a life of faith, our ancestors who lived in remote mountain villages perhaps could experience spirituality more powerfully than Harvard Law School students.

Once I realized this fact, I discovered that even if a person didn't exhibit high intelligence, he or she could still possess a deep spirituality in the understanding of God and the desire to follow his will. I witnessed this in many people, including Joseph.

For this reason, while watching Joseph grow up, I laughed many times at certain incidents, particularly involving Joseph's habit of asking guests to pray. Whenever we had guests over to share a meal, Joseph would always pick one person among the guests and request, "You pray!"

This surprised me because the person he nominated to pray was usually either a pastor or missionary. Truthfully, I didn't think it was a coincidence that he picked those particular people.

So I often told my husband jokingly, "Don't you think Joseph has a keen sense of spirituality? He's usually able to point out a pastor or missionary to say grace." I was half-joking. But after that conversation, my husband and I paid attention to see which person Joseph would pick. The next time we had guests, I was impressed again when he picked a pastor to pray. Joseph had the gift to discern who the faithful servant of the Lord was at the dinner table.

My son was a boy who had to go to church, a boy who yawned loudly during sermons, a boy who sprang up to pass gas because he couldn't hold it, a boy who sat still and worshiped God, and a boy who would never miss an offering. Yes, this boy was Hong-Yul Chung, my first son, Joseph.

Watching Joseph subtly influenced my family. We devoted Sundays to worship and offering tithes to God. In addition, my husband went on mission trips to Africa, China, and Southeast Asia several times a year. To give two-tenths, and sometimes even three-tenths, we volunteered to support many charitable projects, such as digging wells, building orphanages, and helping children in North Korea.

Joseph had such an exemplary spiritual life that he became the model of spirituality for us. Yet his church life was not a programmed routine at all. He didn't go to church because we pushed him or because he had an obligation to do so. Whether about church or service, Joseph had his personal preferences.

■ ■

And he would walk happily on the path he had chosen according to his own standards. In fact, Joseph decided on his own to attend a Canadian church instead of a Korean one.

Joseph was a very friendly and outgoing boy. So he tended to greet whomever he ran into without prejudice. "Hi! How are you? My name is Joseph. What is your name?" Usually in Canadian churches, when Joseph said hello, people didn't hesitate to respond, "Hi, Joseph. How are you?"

However, due to cultural reasons, people in Korean churches are generally more reserved. They didn't know how to treat Joseph how they wanted to. As a result, they either gazed blankly at him or simply didn't respond.

Having experienced this seemingly hostile environment, Joseph demanded one day, "No Korean church!"

Joseph, who was sensitive to how people responded to him, insisted on going exclusively to American or Canadian churches where he felt more welcomed. Joseph felt that Western churches were more open and accepting of people with differences. Consequently, my family often had to serve in two different churches separately. Despite the numerous attempts to attend church together, whether in LA, Seattle, or Vancouver, I had to go to a Korean church to continue serving as a church pianist or choirmaster, whereas Joseph attended Western churches by himself.

After Joseph's thirtieth birthday, my husband decided to take him to a Korean church called Jubilee Chapel because we thought we couldn't have Joseph go to a Canadian church alone forever. Jubilee Chapel was established on the campus of Trinity Western University. Its ministry was mainly for pastors and missionaries, who were on campus to study. Joseph loved going to this small Korean church. What about this congregation of fifty to sixty members captured Joseph's heart? I believe the biggest reason for Joseph's love toward this church had to do with Rev. Seunghoon Yang.

He gave Joseph a special task. "Joseph, would you like to be in charge of the weekly church bulletin?" The church members who treated Joseph like family were a significant factor, but above all, Joseph seemed to enjoy his special mission to come to church early on Sundays and fold bulletins. To fulfill his mission, he strove to meticulously fold each bulletin. Some may wonder what is so significant about folding bulletins. For everyone else, this work is simple and straightforward; but for Joseph, he needed to spend considerable time to finish the job, which he did with utmost care. Every Sunday morning he headed to church with great excitement, never wanting to miss a single day.

In the afternoon, Joseph also attended the Love Ministry at Philadelphia Korean Church. Love Ministry was a worship service designed for students with developmental and intellectual disabilities like Joseph's. This ministry helped children with special needs to walk in faith. The way this church reached these children demonstrated real love. Church members were also very involved in this ministry and at least one volunteer oversaw each child. Joseph must have felt their genuine love for him as well. Every Sunday, he went to Jubilee Chapel in the morning and then went to Love Ministry in

■ ■

the afternoon for worship and other activities like memorizing Bible verses.

He also loved going to Milal School every Saturday, which was a special school run by Rev. Sanghyun Lee for kids with developmental disorders.

Witnessing Joseph, who loved prayer and praise, made it clear to me that his faith in Jesus was purer and truer than mine or anyone's. Joseph experienced heaven through worship and prayer.

⌇

As he entered young adulthood, Joseph became even more passionate about praising God. Joseph especially loved the "Hallelujah Chorus" from Handel's oratorio *Messiah*. Because playing the whole oratorio took two to three hours from beginning to end, I couldn't play all of it for him. Instead I bought him a CD, and Joseph often listened to the entire musical composition.

When Joseph was sad, I would either say, "Joseph, 'Hallelujah'!" or other times I would ask, "Joseph, do you want to sing praises?" Within seconds, Joseph would smile and take me to the piano room. He would pull up a chair next to the piano, ready to sing when I started playing. Joseph had already decided on the list and order of songs. It always began with "While the Lord is my Shepherd." As Joseph sang, "While the Lord is my Shepherd and I'm kept in His care, like a lamb, dear and precious in His sight," he truly looked like a little lamb, peacefully held in the arms of the Lord.

Sheep are known to be very weak in the animal kingdom. Because of their extreme nearsightedness, they can easily become lost while grazing unless there is a shepherd to lead them—the shepherd is indispensable to a flock of sheep. To live, the sheep must follow their shepherd, and the shepherd must protect his flock.

The third verse shows the relationship between the shepherd and the sheep even more clearly: "Evil beasts cannot harm me while my Shepherd is near, nor the wind nor the rain can do me harm. Night and day, He is ready with His arms open here, and I rest in the safety of that arm."

Joseph, who had autism, felt uncomfortable communicating with others even though he certainly had opinions on what he liked and disliked. In this world, communication with others was always a challenge. For Joseph, living in a world filled with misunderstandings was like living with wild animals. Regardless, Joseph kept praising; he was satisfied because he knew the shepherd took care of him. Joseph sang happily, just like King David. King David sang songs of praise even while being hunted; he was not afraid because Jesus was his shepherd.

After this first song, Joseph would sing more hymns like "God Whose Grace Overflows," "I Hear Thy Welcome Voice," "Since Christ My Soul from Sin Set Free," and "I'd Rather Have Jesus," to the third or fourth verses. Sometimes with eyes closed, sometimes with deep solemnity, sometimes while clapping his hands—he sang all the songs he knew from memory. At times he went off pitch or off rhythm, but the

■ ■

beads of perspiration on Joseph's face made it explicit that he praised the Lord with all his heart and might.

The singing of the hymns usually took us about thirty to forty minutes. Then, Joseph, as if he never wanted to forget that he was a proud Korean, sang the national anthem of the Republic of Korea. He sang with great expression. After we were done singing the national anthem, I finally got my breath back. I had reason to be tired after forty minutes of rigorous singing and playing. But, when it came to this moment, Joseph would stare at me without saying a word. With this glance, he sent me a silent message, asking me to play "the song" that would be the grand finale of this session of praise.

"Joseph, it's enough for today. Let's go to sleep." These were the days when I was too tired. Joseph, finally accepting that the time for singing of hymns and the national anthem was over for that day, would return his room.

Other times, when I had a touch more energy, I would say, "Joseph, would you like to hear 'Hallelujah' before going to bed?" A smile would light up his face as he waited for the beautiful and majestic melody to begin.

"Hallelujah, hallelujah ..."

How can I describe the luminous joy on his face when "Hallelujah" played? Sitting silently still as the music drew him, Joseph looked completely satisfied, as if to declare: "This is enough. I am content. I am happy with just being able to praise you, Lord. I glorify your name. Hallelujah!" Having listened to the music with all the joy in the world, he would finally stand up and blurt out one word:

▫ ▫

"Done!"

This meant he was satisfied for praising as much as he wanted that day, and he would again praise Jesus, his beloved shepherd, the next day. This is how Joseph found the source of happiness for life—by praising God.

We celebrated Joseph's first birthday with joyful and blessed hearts, not knowing what his future held.

Joseph loved watching the ocean.

Joseph loved playing in a bathtub with his younger brother.

Joseph taught himself how to swim when he was two years old and always loved playing in the pool.

It was tough to get Joseph in the picture, but we managed!

We used to have pizza in our backyard.

Ms. Tate had been the biggest influence on Joseph's life. Her kindness, dedication, and heart to serve children with special needs were true blessings to us.

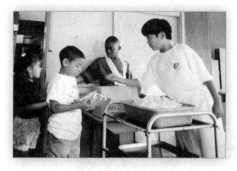

Joseph was a caring soul who always enjoyed serving others.

My heart was filled with gratitude and joy on Joseph's graduation day.

Joseph spent two to three hours daily drawing pictures or transcribing the Bible in his beautiful cursive writing.

Joseph did a fantastic job at his brother's wedding, despite our worries over his seizures.

Joseph at Grandma's gravesite with Grandpa.
Joseph's grandma loved on Joseph and prayed
for him every morning when she was alive.

I received an Honorary Doctorate degree as recognition
for my humanitarian efforts, all because of the blessings I
received through Joseph. This event occurred just a few
months before Joseph suddenly passed away.

Joseph gazing into the distance deep in
thought as if he were looking back on life.

Caleb lovingly touched Joseph's tombstone when we told him his uncle was there.

The first Joe's Table opened in Burnaby, Canada in 2013.

Joe's Table opened the second location at Sarang Church in Seoul, South Korea in 2014.

6

Joseph Is a Missionary

Raising Joseph was exhausting and too much to bear. I can't recall exactly when I started to pray, "God, this boy is not mine but yours. You raise him. I give him to you."

Most parents see their children as "my kids" or "my sons and daughters." I was the same; I had been immersed in how to raise my child well before Joseph was born. I paid attention to what I ate; I put a lot of effort into prenatal care to give birth to a healthy child. As many people do, I felt a great responsibility to mold a good human being, like a potter and his artistic creations.

Blessing me with five children, God gave me the same message for all of them: each is his child, and he will raise them. God made me realize that my children's true father is God, and my husband and I are called to be his servants.

■ ■

If Joseph had not suffered from a developmental disorder, I might not have understood this message. I would have felt like I had fallen short of my expectations. I could have fallen into deep frustration if I had continued to design my children's lives.

However, I realized early on that no matter how hard I tried, I wasn't the one who could move their hearts. All I could do as a parent was acknowledge God's sovereignty over my children and surrender them to him. The best I could do was pray for them. After all, it was up to God to open their eyes, give them a longing for eternity, mature their hearts, and grow their bodies.

Once we admit God's authority and plans for our children, we will no longer compare our children to others'. In other words, if we truly realized that God created our children uniquely, we would see them as precious gifts from God, just as they are. And we would rejoice in seeing our children grow slowly, step by step. It becomes possible to hope for and be pleased with God's good and absolute plans for our children.

When Joseph reached twenty-one, I had become a mother who thought, *Joseph, you make me happy*, every time I saw him. During the time of seemingly endless pain and tears, I don't know why I struggled to think this way. But, when Joseph entered young adulthood, my heart was rooted in faith in God. I could leave Joseph in his hands because I trusted him. I believed Joseph was in his best state when being led by God; therefore, as his mother, I was filled with peace and happiness rather than anxiety and worry.

The toughest days of my life were when we wrestled with Joseph's epilepsy. Because Joseph hated sleeping next to other people, I used to sleep upstairs where my daughters' bedrooms were. My youngest son, Christian, had a bedroom right next to Joseph's. So, when Joseph's seizures would start in the middle of the night, Christian always woke up and ran upstairs, shouting, "Mom! Mom!"

Our oldest children had already left for college, and it should have been my youngest son's, Christian's, turn to finally start receiving all the attention. Instead, Christian became a watchman and guarded his brother every night. Sometimes, he would run to me with tears rolling down his face. I would run down to take care of Joseph with no time to even comfort Christian. Joseph's seizures would stop after some minutes. I would pray for him, but I would still have to wait and make sure he wouldn't have another attack. So, I would stay in Christian's room to wait and fall asleep.

One night, however, I could not fall back to sleep. Although I had witnessed Joseph's seizures numerous times, it still hurt me to see him suffer. That night was especially painful. I thought and wept. *How much better it would be if I could just take his place?*

No words could comfort me. Desperate to know what God wanted to say to me, I opened an English Bible that I found in my son's room. After all, God knew all the circumstances, including Joseph's illness and our pains. My eyes stopped at Jeremiah 29:11. I had known the verse for many years, but that day I couldn't stop staring at it. The translation was different in English: "'For I know the plans I have for you,' declares the Lord, 'plans to prosper you and not to harm you, plans to give you hope and a future.'"

In the Korean translation, the same verse was written, "For I know the *thoughts* I have for you," but the English translation read, "the *plans* I have for you." Suddenly, I felt like I finally found the answer to the question I had had for many years: Does God even have a purpose and a plan for Joseph?

While I reflected on the word "plans," I found myself having a spiritual conversation with the Lord.

I asked him, *Lord,* do you have plans for Joseph?

He answered, *I do, of course. Just as I have plans for you, I have very special plans for Joseph too.*

Later, I heard the same Bible verse again when I attended a church service in Cuba where my husband and I visited during a mission trip. Pastor Davison, a world-renowned preacher from Arizona, gave the sermon. The sermon was based on his testimony after a sudden accident left him paralyzed. He talked about the ministry he had because of his physical disabilities. While listening to the sermon, I was convinced that God had a plan for me as he had for the preacher and certainly for Joseph as well. God's plan gave us hope and a future.

When I came back to the United States, I wrote out this Bible verse in large print and affixed it to the side of Joseph's bed. Even during the hardest times, when Joseph had seizures several times a night, I reminded myself of this promise—that God, who was faithful and loving, had amazing plans for my son.

■ ■ □ ■ □ ■ □ ■ □ ■ □ ■ □ ■ □ ■ □ ■ □ ■ □ ■ □ ■ □ ■ □ ■ □ ■ □ ■ □ ■

From that moment on, things changed. Whenever Joseph woke up from a seizure, I expressed gratitude rather than despair. I was thankful he could begin a new day even after fighting seizures every night. Also, I was thankful his seizures happened at night while he was in bed rather than during the day, which was potentially a lot more dangerous and risky.

Since Joseph had multiple seizures at night, my eyes were always red from staying up with him. In the morning, I would still go to choir practice with bloodshot eyes. I thought the song I sang as I played might be the last song of my life. That made me praise God with all my strength and all my heart. To the Lord who gave my son another day, I wanted to give glory. To the Lord who gave me the gift of today, I wanted to give thanks and praise. As I praised the Lord, all my worries evaporated, and instead I gained a newfound energy and a fountain of joy that made my heart burst.

Life became a constant song of praise. I was alive to welcome a new morning. I could open up my mouth to praise the Lord for the new day. This joy sustained my life.

I learned how to appreciate every day. *Time flies never to return*. In the wilderness, God taught me how precious each day was through Joseph. I praised the Lord who gave me this revelation, and I continued onward, beyond what used to seem like an infinite wilderness.

If I didn't leave Joseph in God's hands, I would be unable to see anything but Joseph for the rest of my life. My life would have been full of trial and tribulation in my struggle to make my son a little better. However, since I believed God was guiding Joseph, this allowed me to make room for volunteer work and music.

For that reason, I had the opportunity to play as an accompanist in various concerts. One opportunity was a charity concert at Vancouver's Massey Theatre, which was held when Joseph was about twenty-one years old. Joy Center organized the concert to help people with disabilities. It featured an internationally acclaimed soprano, Youngmi Kim, and a violinist, Dr. In-Hong Cha. Dr. In-Hong Cha, known as the "Maestro in a Wheelchair," had become the first disabled music professor at an American university, Wright State University.

Weeks before the concert, media interviews were scheduled for promotional purposes. Because Youngmi Kim and Dr. In-Hong Cha were in Korea and America, respectively, many of the local journalists in Vancouver wanted to interview me.

During an interview, a journalist first asked me about my family. I figured she asked me this to relieve the stress of the interview and make me feel comfortable. Unlike past experiences, I started talking comfortably about my children, including Joseph.

"So your first son is twenty-one. Is he in college?"

I responded to the question with a smile and a shake of the head.

"No, my first son doesn't go to school. He graduated from a high school for special kids. But he is the biggest blessing to me and an angel who delivers God's message to my family."

The interviewer was astonished and wanted to know more about Joseph. Starting from his birth, I told stories about my frustration and discouragement after discovering Joseph's disability and the challenges I had gone through after Joseph's accident. Then I shared some information about the concert and ended the interview.

The next day, the column in the newspaper shocked me. It was supposed to promote the concert, but instead, the article featured Joseph and me in huge letters. I thought the interviewer had asked all these questions about my family because she was just curious. How odd that my family's story would be in a non-Christian newspaper, laid out like a testimony.

That was the first time my family's story was published. Shortly after the publication of my interview, someone who loved and cared about my family called and shared his worries. He worried that the story of Joseph might negatively impact my other children. Having never thought of it that way, I called my youngest brother, Paul Lee, who was a pastor in Los Angeles at the time. He was the youngest, but he always offered me warm words of encouragement and spiritual guidance. I asked him for his thoughts.

"Do you think I shouldn't have talked about Joseph?"

In response to my question, he said, "Sister, I am happy for you."

"What? Happy?"

"Yes. Being able to put Joseph's story in a newspaper means you've accepted him as he is, which in turn means your wounds are healed. I am happy for that. Good for you."

Hearing these words, I gained some strength. However, at that point, I didn't expect God's plan to unfold the way it did through Joseph's story.

■ ■

As soon as I hung up the phone, I received another call from an unknown woman who told me she had read the article and obtained my contact information from the newspaper. She was a young immigrant mother who was raising an autistic child as well. Just hearing her voice made my heart break. People will never know the immense challenges of raising a disabled child in a foreign country with no friends or relatives, unless they have walked that path. This poor mother's heart must have been broken, having no one to confide in for support. Also, she had no solution for how to help her child overcome the culture shock at school. As a parent who had walked in her shoes, I first wanted her to shed all the tears she had stored up deep inside her heart.

"You must be exhausted. Why don't we meet?"

We did just that. I met her as well as two other Korean mothers. It had been over twenty years since I left Korea, but it was my first time meeting other Korean mothers with autistic children.

The moment we met, we were instantly hugging and crying. Their tears seeped into my heart as if they were my own siblings. As our tales and tears continued, we discovered an amazing fact. Even though we had only met for the first time, we understood one another completely; we even knew how to perfectly counsel and comfort each other.

A heart that can empathize with others' suffering is not given to everyone. Only the people who have personally experienced the sorrow, who have stood under the spotlight of being ridiculed, or who have been afflicted by the same illness can truly empathize. Upon meeting one another, we realized that we have been given this ability to empathize with the pain and suffering of our own powerlessness and feelings of rejection.

An instant bond formed among us as we finally learned there were others who understood our pain and we were no longer alone. All of us wanted to help others who were also in pain. Our three-hour conversation brought us so close it seemed like we had been friends for thirty years. We felt a sudden overwhelming attachment to each other.

Because it was time to pick up our kids from school, we had to end our time together, but we were already looking forward to our next meeting. The next time we gathered, a few more mothers showed up, then again a few more. Every time we got together, our stories turned into prayers overcoming sorrow and gratitude overcoming pain.

Officially, our gathering became the Bethesda Parents Society that held weekly meetings. It has been twelve years since we gathered as a community to serve immigrant families with disabled children. In retrospect, if anyone had asked me to organize such a group, I would have probably avoided responsibility because I felt overburdened and fearful. But God, who knew me better than anyone, authored the series of events from Joseph's story appearing in a newspaper to the mothers reading the article, which led to our meeting and to the establishment of the Bethesda Parents Society to spiritually build up many families. The Bethesda mothers continue to meet on a weekly basis.

■ ■

There are no coincidences for God. According to Jesus, "Not one [sparrow] will fall to the ground outside your Father's care" (Matthew 10:29). It was a part of God's perfect plan to use the article and Joseph like a seed. He planted Bethesda Parents Society in October 2003 to take away the pain of lonely people living in the margins of society.

Bethesda Parents Society strives to be a community open to anyone. Therefore, from the beginning, we kept our doors open to any mother raising a disabled child, regardless of their religious background. However, as it was a God-initiated meeting in the first place, we focused on how to encounter and walk with God in our daily lives. As a result, our time together was filled with Bible studies, participation in volunteer work, and practical seminars on parenting.

Some may question why we would need to get involved in extra volunteer work when we had to deal with our own children. I can understand why people would wonder. When you look into the households of families with autistic children and listen to their stories of endless toil, by no means would they have room in their lives to do anything else. Considering their circumstances, almost every family can rightfully challenge others, "If anyone is going through more trials than we are, please step forward."

Some autistic children also suffer from OCD (obsessive compulsive disorder). Some autistic children are susceptible to epileptic seizures. Some have serious sleep problems that deprive their parents of sleep. Some autistic children can go to regular schools while others cannot. Moreover, mothers of these children, no matter where in the world they live, are forced to embrace extreme loneliness, unable to relieve the pain in their hearts.

Therefore, I wanted Bethesda Parents Society to be a haven where we could talk frankly about our weaknesses and stress. Just as I had wished, our meetings were exactly what I had hoped from the beginning. Whether we discussed issues related to toilet training, eating, or problems at school, we boldly exposed our weaknesses and vulnerabilities. In response, the mothers demonstrated sympathy to each other's struggles. When a mother brought a new issue to light, we put our heads together to find a solution.

What happened during Bethesda meetings was totally opposite to what one would expect at typical Korean gatherings. At high school or college reunions, for instance, the discussions usually revolve around people's achievements. People want to know whose children are at the best universities and whose husband earns the higher salary. During such conversations of comparisons and competition, only the mother whose child was admitted to a top university or a wife whose husband makes the most money enjoys the spotlight while the others hide their insecurities in the shadows.

However, at Bethesda gatherings, it was the opposite. When a mother brought up a troublesome issue, another mother would join in the conversation. "Well, my child is even worse. We are going through the same problems." During our meetings, the person enduring the greatest challenge became the star of the day! When that mother shared her burden, the others were relieved of their heavy hearts by praying together for that mother.

I've found a Scripture that expresses this well: "If I must boast, I will boast of the things that show my weakness" (2 Corinthians 11:30). As the Bible verse teaches us, when we boast of the things that show our weaknesses, it binds together our broken hearts. The more we discover our weaknesses, the more we learn to pray and depend on God instead of relying on our own strength. And as we pray for the weakest among us, we can expect great things, which God will reveal through and in us.

The mothers who boast in their weaknesses, who look after the weak and pray for them—these are the mothers of Bethesda.

"Let's go volunteer to help others!" I often insisted. Though we may be the very ones who need care and support from society, we ought to reach out to the weak first. When weak people like us go out into the world and help the broken, we will wipe away tears—not only theirs but also ours.

⌒

While raising Joseph, I came to realize that all the things we enjoy, live with, and take for granted are actually given to us because of God's great mercy. It's a gift from God to be able to speak and walk on two legs.

I also regarded my musical talent as God's special gift. When we first moved to Seattle, I wanted to serve neighbors in need with this talent. I wondered who would be the loneliest people and whose hearts needed the comfort of music most. I went to an elderly care home and played the piano while Joseph went to school.

After I moved to White Rock Beach, I tried again to find an elderly care home, but in Canada, I had to go through a complicated verification process to become a volunteer. While figuring out what to do, I heard there was a Korean women's choir consisting of approximately twenty seniors. It was called Zion Mission Choir and they gathered in the basement of a church. The choir was conducted and run by Shin-Ok Kim, who was the mother of Young-Soo Lim, the former pastor of Young-rak Church in Seoul, Korea.

I met with the choir because I had a desire to help them, as well as to learn from Shin-Ok Kim. I admired her character and her endless passion for praising in spite of her old age. The choir members were very grateful that I volunteered to be an accompanist.

These ladies poured out their love for me. They always seemed to look forward to seeing me and treated me warmly. Of course, I went there to serve and give; however, I received more from their happy faces and abundant grace. I always came home with much more than I had given. I was convicted over and over that anyone could be healed from a broken heart while praising God.

After Shin-Ok Kim retired, I took charge of conducting the choir. Joseph sometimes came and sat in the back to listen to our singing. While conducting, I gained so much strength just by looking at Joseph. So, on the days Joseph visited rehearsals with me, my face always burst into a smile. The choir members loved Joseph so much—they took pictures with him and even brought him food.

"Joseph, come up and let's praise," is what someone would say to encourage Joseph. He would come forward and sing his favorite song like "While the Lord Is My Shepherd."

When he wasn't with me, the choir members often asked about Joseph. One of them observed, "This is how I realized how much you love Joseph. You look more energetic whenever you talk about him. You seem like the happiest person in the world."

Yes, Joseph was my joy. And it was the time spent with Zion Mission Choir that provided me with greater strength to raise him and rejoice. While serving the choir, I learned that I gained more energy and joy by using my talent and time to serve others rather than resting during the few hours that my children were in school.

This experience helped me encourage the Bethesda mothers to go out and serve others.

Thankfully, the mothers in my group knew the meaning of the phrase "go out and serve others" better than anyone else. Everyone actively participated in volunteer activities at least once a month. We sometimes collected recyclables or used items and sold them to help the homeless. We also visited and took care of lonely elders or other disabled children. The surprising thing is that the mothers could take care of their own children with more heart and strength once they started volunteering. Everyone realized that they gained more strength and energy once they left their own children in God's hands and committed a mere ten to twenty percent of their time and talent to taking care of others.

While many organizations tended to focus on programs for the disabled, I felt a strong need to bring healing and education to the parents of these children. I did so not only because of their great distress but also because a parent's recovery was essential to raising a healthy child.

In fact, mothers of autistic children carry many wounds and scars. They ask, "Why are these things happening to me?" and "What should my child and I live for?" I had also been discouraged for many years, not able to find the answers to these haunting questions. Nothing in the world had offered me a convincing answer.

I finally found what I had been looking for from the Word of God—the God who created the universe and all mankind:

As he [Jesus] went along, he saw a man blind from birth. His disciples asked him, "Rabbi, who sinned, this man or his parents, that he was born blind?"

"Neither this man nor his parents sinned," said Jesus, "but this happened so that the works of God might be displayed in him." (John 9:1–3)

Even in ancient times, as soon as the disciples saw a blind man, they asked Jesus the same haunting question: Why did this happen to him? Much to the disciples' disappointment,

Jesus stated that it was neither because of the man's parents' sin nor his own. Simply, Jesus' words shed light on the destiny of the blind man "that the works of God might be displayed in him."

This Scripture gives us wisdom on how to understand pain and suffering in our lives. Since we cannot simply attribute suffering to anyone's sin, we should not strain to figure out a root cause in the time of suffering. Rather, we should strive to see how it will reveal God's glory. After all, the reason why this man was born blind was a part of God's grand plan—to display his divine work through him.

"Why did this happen to me?"

"What should my child and I live for?"

Jesus' answer to these questions is simple and clear. Our children are born to display the glory of God, who turns mourning into dancing, sorrow into songs of joy, worries into gratitude, and hatred into love. They are destined to live for his glory. Once I realized the meaning of this Scripture, I shared it with the Bethesda mothers to encourage them and to reinforce that our children are special and precious and that God will certainly reveal his glorious work through them.

A few days later, Jihwan's mother (who was the secretary of Bethesda Parents Society) came to talk to me. "All along, I thought my son's disability was due to the sins of my past lives. So I always struggled with guilt and pain. Then, when I met these mothers who believe in Jesus, they were so different. They saw the situation from a totally different perspective: the children's disability is neither due to God's mistake nor their mothers' wrongdoings in a previous life. They believed it was for the glory of God and rejoiced in their suffering. Do you think I could be like them too?"

She was the same person who had said, "Umm, I don't say this kind of prayer because I have a different religion" when I suggested we pray before the meal when we first met. Now I heard this person confessing, "I want to live like those Christian mothers."

Can you imagine how happy I was? I recommended she read *The Purpose Driven Life*, a book by Rick Warren, and suggested she join the Bible study.

Not long after, something amazing happened. Reading through the Bible, she eventually came to believe in Jesus Christ as her Savior. The story doesn't end here. As soon as she started her faith journey, she showed the greatest passion for sharing the Gospel to newcomers. One day, she even made a radical decision. "Both my parents and in-laws have not heard about Jesus yet. I believe in him now, and I am living in joy. I must go to Korea and deliver this good news of salvation to my parents."

Though she had only recently become a believer, she went all the way to Korea to share the Gospel with her parents and siblings. We couldn't help but be shocked and moved by her conviction.

She continued growing as a believer who would recognize Christ in every instance of her life, and we all agreed this verse was intended for someone like her: "Many who are first will be last, and many who are last will be first" (Matthew 19:30).

One day, this same mother, who was now a living testimony of Bethesda, came up to me out of the blue and proclaimed, "Stephanie, I think Joseph is a missionary. Without Joseph, Bethesda wouldn't have existed, and I wouldn't know Jesus for my whole life. I came here and believed Jesus because of Joseph. He is a missionary."

When I heard that Joseph was a missionary, I bowed in amazement.

"Joseph is a missionary" was the prayer of my husband and me—the vow we made to the Lord—that we had never told a single soul. We prayed, "This first child you have given us, we will raise him as a pastor or missionary."

Having said this prayer in God's presence, I could not have told anyone about it after discovering Joseph's disability. It was unimaginable that my child could be a missionary with his disabilities. Now God spoke to me through this new believer, letting me know his master plan for Joseph.

I prayed, "Yes, God. You are calling Joseph to be the missionary to my family and to other families with disabled children. Joseph led my family and the Bethesda mothers closer to you. We think we have to be wise and intelligent to do your work, but you call the weakest and smallest to spread the Gospel."

God's promise to us in Jeremiah 29:11 was becoming a reality. God had a special plan for Joseph. I could barely take in the overflowing joy and peace pouring out of this truth.

7

Independence and Faithfulness

How can we comprehend the breadth and depth of God's infinite wisdom with our tiny, little minds? As I came to understand a fragment of his plan, the wonders of divine providence rendered me speechless.

Above all, in a world that does not willingly accept Jesus, it was incredible to discover how the Gospel bore fruit through Joseph, who could barely speak. I came to know how blessed Joseph's life was. What is a mother's ultimate wish for her children? Wouldn't it be to reveal God's glory, rejoice in him, be joyful, and live forever with Jesus in heaven? Rather than merely living a limited existence in the physical world, Joseph rejoiced in God, fulfilling his divine destiny, and stood on the road leading to the heavenly kingdom.

In a world full of lies, fraud, and deceit, the children of Bethesda were full of innocence and truth. Children like Joseph do not know anything about telling a lie, holding a malicious intention, or having an insincere heart. Looking into their innocent eyes, I often said to the Bethesda mothers, "God must reserve the best seats in heaven for our children."

Suffering is not the only thing that children's autism causes in their parents' lives. In fact, because of their disability, these special children don't eagerly jump into the vices of the world. Through my experience, I realized their autism gave them a huge advantage in God's kingdom. As a result, we found peace of mind and rejoiced rather than cried about our children's innocent and forthright behavior.

For instance, one day when we were having dinner with a pastor, Joseph stood up from his chair to pass gas.

The pastor remarked, "Hey, Joseph. I envy you. I envy how you can break wind anytime and anywhere you want."

His statement caused everyone to burst out laughing (harder than you can imagine). We came to love Joseph's silly behaviors because of his pure innocence and genuine expressions—so different from "normal" people. I loved him just the way he was.

Joseph's life was filled with proof of God's purpose for mankind. Joseph gave himself to God as a blank canvas for God to paint his glory on.

Joseph was so precious to me that I would hold his hand and introduce him to everyone. Whenever I introduced Joseph to people, my heart would shout, "Look! Here is my precious son!"

I kept sending this message to Joseph. "Joseph, you are a missionary. You are such a precious child whom God sent to this world with a very special plan."

Joseph seemed to know that people saw him in this light, and he started to change day by day. His compulsive behavior disappeared. During puberty, he used to clean and tidy up everything incessantly. He would even clip his nails so near to the skin that his fingers and toes would bleed. This broke my heart, but he couldn't stand it when I wouldn't let him clip his nails.

These behaviors were gone once he stepped into adulthood. He became a gentle lamb.

Wherever he went, Joseph acted like a gentleman. If the chairs weren't placed in a line, he would straighten them. If he saw garbage on the floor, he would pick it up and put it in the trash. Whomever he met, he cheerfully greeted with a gentle smile, "Hi, how are you? My name is Joseph. What is your name?" Joseph was no longer the boy who couldn't sit still for even a few seconds.

These changes in Joseph came during my time at Bethesda Parents Society. From this pivotal point, the second turning point of his life, Joseph transformed into his new nickname, "gentleman." Joseph had truly become a gentleman—a strong young man who resembled a flower in bloom.

As we introduced Joseph to people, my husband and I received many gifts. One of them was the gift of being able to tear down walls between people.

My husband occasionally meets important people during

■ ■

his business abroad. One day, he met with a high-profile politician. My husband casually brought up Joseph's story while he talked about our family. This caused the politician to open up about his own concerns for his adolescent child.

After the conversation, they developed a friendship that went beyond business. Later, when the politician's wife came to Vancouver, she visited my home. We prayed together and encouraged each other; our families became friends.

I can recall another incident a few years ago. I took Joseph with me to visit a homeless support center that was run by one of my pastor friends. I knew the name of the place but didn't have the specific address. I headed to Hastings Street where a large population of homeless people in Vancouver reside. Lost, I stopped to look for a sign.

Suddenly, Joseph vanished, and I couldn't find him.

Startled, I searched for Joseph among the homeless people. I was suddenly seized with fear that there could be alcoholics and drug addicts in the group. But Joseph walked up to them, fearless.

He stopped in front of a homeless man and held out his hand, "Hi! How are you? My name is Joseph. What is your name?"

Fear paralyzed me. *What if this man harms Joseph?* I had an urge to run and take him away, but not knowing what to do, I just stood and watched. There seemed to be an awkward silence between Joseph, who asked for a handshake, and the man, who stared at Joseph blankly. I swallowed.

Suddenly, a smile appeared on the homeless man's face

as he extended his arm to reach Joseph's hand. "My name is Peter." The response made Joseph smile. Then, Joseph walked back to me as a man who had completed his mission; the man who shook Joseph's hand continued to smile.

Watching Joseph walk toward me, without knowing what he had done, made me think: *Joseph, we tend to categorize people and judge them based on their looks. But you hold out your hand to anyone without prejudice. Yes, Joseph. That was the heart of Jesus. Jesus went up to anyone first and said, "My name is Jesus. What is your name?" He wants us to open our doors and follow him, holding his hands. Joseph, you are teaching me the heart of Jesus, who comes to us first and knocks on our door and waits …*

This revelation deeply moved me, and I realized once more what a great blessing Joseph was. *If it weren't for Joseph, what kind of person would I have become?* But Joseph guided me to see the heart of Jesus, who loves us so much. I gave Joseph a thumbs-up as he walked back to me with a big smile on his face.

"Joseph, you are the best! You are mom's best teacher." My compliment encouraged him even more, and Joseph looked proud. I too proudly marched down the street, holding Joseph's hand tightly.

Even with his simple ability to greet people first, Joseph became a peacemaker to many. This ability shone even brighter in the waiting rooms of the hospital's department of neurosurgery.

When Joseph had earned his nickname "gentleman," he was still wrestling with seizures. As a result, Joseph and I often visited the hospital. Every time we sat in the waiting room, my heart sank. I realized I was not the only one who felt the sadness. The other patients and parents dealing with brain-related injuries sat in heavy silence. A chill filled the air. But Joseph was different. No matter which hospital or which neurosurgery waiting room he entered, he walked among the depressed and asked them for a handshake one by one. "Hi! How are you? My name is Joseph. What is your name?"

As Joseph broke the silence with his signature greeting, patients and parents responded to his sudden gesture. "My name is Tom."

Then Joseph would move on to the next person.

"Hi! How are you? My name is Joseph. What is your name?"

"My name is William."

Soon, the people in the waiting room would start to smile. After all, it's difficult to say "hello" without a smile. Eventually, the people in the waiting room began to remember each other's names. Thanks to Joseph, the waiting room became more like a cafe, where people exchanged greetings and chatted.

"How are you, Tom?"

"William, why are you in the hospital today?"

Once the gloomy waiting area turned into a friendly place, Joseph would return to his seat as though he had just finished his job. Then he would wait quietly for his name to be called.

These times reminded me of this verse, "Blessed are the peacemakers, for they will be called children of God" (Matthew 5:9).

This Scripture was being realized in Joseph's life. Joseph,

the gentleman, bred friendship everywhere he went. Having the ability to greet people with a pure heart without prejudice, Joseph had now become a "peacemaker."

⌐

Major changes came into our lives when we met Young-Ji Na, a teacher from the Milal School where Joseph went every Saturday. After meeting her, Joseph spent a couple of days with the teacher's family when I had to travel abroad. Then we began transitioning into Joseph living with the teacher's family for an entire week and coming home on weekends to be with us. Around that time, in the hopes of building a community for people with disabilities like Joseph, we had purchased a large ranch, which had three separate houses to accommodate Joseph, the Nas, and a special education teacher who would lead the disability program.

This was the answer to my longtime prayer to find the best way for Joseph to live independently. Many Canadian parents encourage their children of approximately twenty to live independently whether or not they have a disability. In addition, this was a solution to a concern I had as a parent: *What will happen to Joseph after I am gone?* I was thankful that, just as I had prayed, Joseph met a kind Korean teacher who cared for him, a teacher with whom he could speak Korean and enjoy Korean food.

Living with his teachers on this ranch, Joseph enjoyed many daily activities. These included bicycling, playing badminton, and swimming. A pastor, who had been praying for Joseph, taught him to play the electronic harp.

Since Joseph was living with his teachers, I could attend early morning prayer services at a church near my home during the weekdays. Although I had longed to go for a while, I couldn't because Joseph required constant care. Looking back, I think God was preparing me to set my eyes on the kingdom of God from this time on. Whenever I kneeled to pray these early mornings, I began by lifting up Joseph and the Bethesda children.

"I lift up these children to your mighty hand, O Lord. You are the loving Shepherd who cares for them. Please guide their ways."

Around this time, Joseph was also moving closer to God by transcribing the Bible. His teacher and I encouraged him to do this after seeing his beautiful cursive writing. It began with a children's Bible, and then she encouraged him to write the entire book of Psalms.

Can Joseph write all 150 Psalms? I was worried because his writing process seemed like hard labor. As he wrote each letter of each word, his writing slowed and his posture became more hunched.

Despite my worries, Joseph took great care in writing out each word and every punctuation mark. He enjoyed doing it so much that he began his day with transcribing the Psalms. In the early days, he lost himself in handwriting for seven hours a day. Then, one day, after he told me his hand hurt, he made the decision to limit the writing to one page a day. Perhaps even he thought writing the Bible for seven hours was too much.

Joseph's cursive writing of the book of Psalms

For Joseph to stay focused on a task was amazing, especially when that task was something mundane by normal standards. Letter by letter, he made every effort to copy each word. If he found a mistake, he rewrote the word with utmost care. When I watched Joseph pouring his heart into each verse, I wondered if there was some secret behind each word.

Throughout this period, Joseph also grappled with severe pain due to his seizures. On days when he had had several seizures during the previous night, he struggled to concentrate on anything. Even on these mornings, Joseph would still begin the day by writing his Psalms. Of course, on those difficult days, he made more spelling mistakes, skipped a few verses, or wrote the same verse repeatedly. However, as soon as he discovered his mistakes, he corrected each one. When

I flip through Joseph's Bible notebook now, I can trace the marks of Joseph's perseverance where he repeatedly wrote, erased, and rewrote words to perfection.

Why didn't Joseph give up on writing the book of Psalms when faced with such great challenges? When I watched Joseph spending two to three hours writing the Bible, I thought of David. Through his psalms, David lifted his loneliness and suffering to God, even as he went into hiding from King Saul. Joseph too may have poured out his own loneliness and suffering to God through transcribing the Psalms.

Joseph was at the pinnacle of his life when he transcribed the book of Psalms. In the spring of 2012, he finally finished copying all 150 Psalms with his beautiful handwriting.

The book of Psalms was transcribed letter by letter with all of Joseph's strength and devotion, as if it were the confession of his faith. Though it took a year and a half of arduous daily effort, the book was finally completed—it would be his life's final project.

8

A Stepping-Stone

In 2012, my family actively started looking for ways to treat Joseph's seizures. To that end, Joseph stayed in a hospital in the United States for a month to see if he could have surgery. The doctors decided it was extremely risky to operate on Joseph as the abnormal brain cells causing the seizures were spread throughout his brain. Of course, I was extremely disappointed, but fortunately they suggested new medication. From that point on, to determine the right balance for him, we reduced the dosage of his previous medication and gradually increased the dosage of the new medication.

After switching to his new medication, Joseph seemed a lot better. At one point, he stopped having seizures for two whole weeks, which made me wonder, *Is Joseph completely cured?* Disappointingly, Joseph began having seizures again, and even had a severe one in the daytime. Not having seizures at night at least gave him a good night's sleep; however, having seizures in the day was very dangerous, so I looked for ways to prevent them.

Our family home was undergoing renovations, so we began living in Joseph's house for six months. The ranch we envisioned to house a community of people with disabilities was a beautiful and peaceful place. There were lakes full of fish and meadows with cows feeding on grass.

The spring and summer we spent with Joseph was a special gift. Joseph especially seemed to enjoy the extra time he spent with his father. My husband had always been busy with his business and couldn't spend a lot of time with Joseph. And now, he wanted to take Joseph with him everywhere he went and was never hesitant to share Joseph's story.

Peter strove to be a missionary who supported other missionaries. But he wrestled with guilt about the story in the Bible about the woman who offered all she had—two small copper coins—to God. To avoid being arrogant in how he treated others and to ensure he rightfully used God's gifts, he was acutely self-aware, even self-critical.

Because of Joseph, Peter knew the heart of Jesus better. Over the six months we lived with Joseph, Peter and Joseph especially enjoyed taking walks on Saturday mornings, their exclusive father-and-son time. Cherry blossoms decorated the trail in front of our house in spring. Joseph loved riding his bike (his father had taught him) and walking through the wildflowers that bloomed every season. The unforgettable moments this father and son made together shone like portraits of heaven.

■ □ ■ □ ■ □ ■ □ ■ □ ■ □ ■ □ ■ □ ■ □ ■ □ ■ □ ■ □ ■ □ ■ □ ■ □ ■ □ ■ □ ■ □ ■

Around this time, a significant event occurred in Joseph's life. Joseph met a girl through Circle of Friends, a program that encouraged meaningful fellowship among adults with disabilities. Her name was Rachel. This pretty Canadian girl fell in love with Joseph when she saw him smile; it was love at first sight. Unlike Joseph, who had an intellectual disability, Rachel had a physical one (she was a paraplegic). Her magnetic personality allowed her to candidly express her feelings for Joseph.

Joseph seemed to like Rachel too. When Rachel came by his side and held his hand quietly, he didn't resist; he would simply stand still and smile. One Valentine's Day, the Circle of Friends' teacher and Joseph's caregiver helped Joseph arrange a surprise for Rachel. He gave Rachel roses and chocolates. Rachel was so happy that she wrote a poem for Joseph. The poem described perfectly a woman's feelings of love for a man:

Joseph, my everything and my happiness
Every moment I look forward to the day I see you.

Joseph did not have the verbal ability to express his understanding of the meaning of these words, but whenever he received her poems, he seemed to comprehend that she loved him. He especially appreciated the fact that a woman was deeply in love with him.

When his siblings asked him, "Joseph, who is your girlfriend?" he would laugh and shout, his neck veins bulging, "R ... Rachel!"

During this special summer of 2012, contentment filled my heart just looking at Joseph. Although he still struggled against frequent seizures, no disability would stop him from being the best gentleman. First, he was enjoying his life; second, he was meek and gentle toward anyone he met. Last but not least, he loved and was being loved.

Any darkness in my mind disappeared with even a glimpse of Joseph's bright face.

"Joseph has grown up the best. He is the least troublesome among us," I often told my family. Indeed, thirty-two-year-old Joseph was living the best time of his life, like the trees in front of our home whose leaves danced for the sky to see.

⌁

"It's the first day of Special Olympics classes. Joseph's feeling fantastic."

September 26, 2012, Wednesday afternoon, I received this text message from Joseph's caregiver. Joseph, who preferred to swim with other people rather than to swim alone, had been looking forward to this class all summer long. His latest nickname, "Seal," perfectly suited him. I imagined him playing in the water for two or three hours.

I was so grateful for these days. Joseph spent a day with us at our newly renovated house and the rest of the week under the care of his teacher. That September morning, I was told Joseph was headed to the pool after he finished writing John 10:13. He had been working on transcribing the book of John.

Joseph must be having a fun time, I thought to myself. That evening, I attended a fundraising concert in West Vancouver. The concert was about to begin when my cell phone's ring broke the silence. I quickly pushed "Answer."

"Hello?" I whispered, worried the concert would begin.

It was his teacher's voice. "Joseph has drowned!"

Confused, I assumed she meant he had a seizure. "What? What happened?" I stood and worked my way to the back of the auditorium.

"We took him out of the pool."

It was fortunate they took him out. The only reason Joseph would have a problem in the water was a seizure. But, still, I thought it wouldn't be a problem if he were taken out immediately.

But the sound from the other end of the phone felt heavy.

I needed more information. "How is he doing now?"

"He is being taken to a hospital."

The teacher's uneasiness caused worry to creep to my chest, but I reasoned it away. I knew I needed to hurry to the hospital.

I wondered why they took Joseph to the hospital. Although it was very dangerous for him to have a seizure in the water, the hospital could do nothing for him after he woke up. *Hmm, it would be better if they just took him home and let him rest.*

Around this period, I had decided to switch Joseph back to the previous medication, because it was too dangerous for him to have seizures during the day. Fortunately, the next day, we had an appointment with the world's leading authority on epilepsy. *I'll ask him about this.*

Due to traffic, it took me one and a half hours to get to the hospital. Meanwhile, my husband called to tell me he would meet me at the hospital. He was packing for a business trip to Korea the next day, so I convinced him not to come. "We will be home soon, anyway."

When I entered the hospital, the staff working with Joseph seemed tense. They wouldn't let me see my son. Something about their elusiveness scared me, and a terrible, sinking feeling grasped me. "What's wrong with Joseph?" I asked the nurse. "Didn't he get taken out of the water after the seizure?"

She shook her head.

"How long was he in the water then?" My voice rose, panicked.

She said she didn't know.

How could they not know?

"I'm sorry. No one knows how much time passed from the beginning of the seizure to his rescue."

What? Where were the teachers? The other kids?

"I've been told they found him at the bottom of the pool."

The nurse's compassionate look didn't help me. My heart collapsed. I could barely stand.

There were two lifeguards at the pool, a Special Olympics swimming coach and Joseph's caregiver. How could they not have seen Joseph having a seizure in the water?

Was he still breathing when they pulled him out? This question came to my mind, but I was too afraid to ask.

I called my husband. He frantically rushed all the way from downtown Vancouver, which was an hour away. After he arrived, we didn't say one word; we just prayed desperately, paced anxiously, and waited for Joseph to wake up.

Eventually, a doctor told us something completely unexpected. According to him, even though Joseph was in the emergency room, nothing could be done. Joseph had to be transferred to another hospital, but no other hospitals would accept him.

What was happening? What did they mean they couldn't do anything? Terrified by the doctor's words, I ran into Joseph's room. "Joseph, Joseph!"

I desperately shouted his name. Joseph was in bed. He had tubes all over his body.

I was so shocked that I couldn't even close my mouth. Then someone explained to me what had happened.

After rescuing Joseph, the lifeguard did CPR and pushed his chest too hard, breaking his rib; this pierced his lungs and caused internal bleeding. To think about Joseph being alone when he endured such extreme pain broke my heart. But I had to pull myself together. It couldn't be the end. Joseph came back to life after he almost drowned when he was nine years old. Joseph endured the struggle of autism, seizures, and OCD. Joseph faced the best season of his life with the realization that he was created to serve God.

Oh God! This isn't the end, right? Lord, please save Joseph. Raise him up.

Shouting and praying inwardly, I clutched my dying heart

and waited for miraculous news. Instead, after some time, a doctor came to say, "I am afraid it's time for you to come and say goodbye."

What?

I couldn't understand him. I was going out of my mind. I moved closer to Joseph.

"But we can take him to another hospital, right? Where they can help him?"

"His organs have stopped working."

This meant he stopped breathing as well. I couldn't believe it. I wanted to shout that it wasn't true. Looking at Joseph's face, it looked like he was sleeping. Blood covered his whole body, but his face appeared clean as if he had just washed it. Who could say this boy was dead?

I heard someone weeping from afar and couldn't decide what to do. Not saying a word, I kept staring at Joseph's face. I saw a teardrop in the corner of his firmly closed left eye. The tear was almost dried up.

Joseph, you were crying too …

The lingering teardrop meant he was alive after he was rescued from the pool. It meant he was crying alone when given CPR or even when in the emergency room. Staring at the teardrop, it felt like someone was stabbing my heart. It was unbearable.

Joseph, open your eyes. Look at me with your eyes. I am here. Your mom is here. Please wake up, Joseph … "Joseph!"

As I shouted my son's name, everything around me became a blur. I heard people moaning loudly and saw Joseph on the bed covered in blood. I even watched the hospital attendants cover him with a white sheet. It all seemed like a scene from a movie, as if it were happening to someone else.

At 12:30 a.m., Joseph left. I couldn't see his pure and beautiful eyes again; I couldn't say goodbye. Joseph left us with his words locked in his chest, where they had always been.

I left the hospital.

Even after I got home, my mind still wandered. *How can Joseph die? How can he leave before I did?* It didn't make sense. All along, I worried about what would happen to Joseph when I was gone; I never thought he would leave me first.

I had no clue how I could carry on. I was utterly lost. I sat there, motionless, when I suddenly heard a new mail notification. The email was from a missionary in China, someone I hadn't heard from in a while.

"Any good news for Joseph?"

No words came. Why did the missionary send this e-mail at this exact time? I had just returned from the hospital and, besides family members, I had not told anyone.

I continued to read the e-mail. "Any good news for Joseph? I had a dream about him last night. Joseph had no disability and his face shone exceptionally brightly. Clad in a nice brown suit, he was gazing at you. You also looked beautiful in a pink two-piece suit. You and Joseph were hugging. And Joseph looked at you with such a loving and proud face, as if he were telling you, 'Thank you, Mom. Thank you for all your love and hard work.' This is why I was wondering about Joseph. Is he getting married?"

The e-mail lifted a curtain for me; I saw his death not as a tragic ending but the stepping-stone to a better place. While we lived in tremendous pain, Joseph enjoyed a true homecoming in heaven. Maybe he was even wearing a nice brown suit with a smile filling his disability-free, bright face.

I opened my eyes, blindfolded by grief, and began to repeat desperately in my heart: *He is gone. Joseph … to heaven. Joseph is in heaven.*

9

Count Your Blessings

Joseph's funeral included the many people who loved him. Pastor Ross Hastings, Joseph's favorite pastor, shared a few words. Rev. Si-Woo Chung, Joseph's grandfather, gave the benediction. And since Joseph loved praising God, the funeral service overflowed with songs of praise.

Our good friend Bramwell Tovey, the music director of the Vancouver Symphony Orchestra, conducted both the Zion Missionary Choir and Grace Community Church Choir to sing Handel's "Hallelujah," Joseph's favorite. While the choirs performed "Hallelujah," I imagined Joseph jumping up any minute from the crowd to join in.

Lying in the casket, Joseph's face looked so peaceful compared to the rest of us who were overcome with grief. He looked like someone who had gone someplace wonderful, and not even a trace of fear was found on his signature carefree face. Joseph was buried across the street from Peace Portal Alliance Church, his favorite church. Buried with him in his casket was his green-covered Bible, the one he carried every time he went to church.

There is a Korean saying that parents bury their child in their hearts when the child dies first. I discovered that no parents ever let go of their child, even once the child has passed. Wherever I went, whatever I did, I always thought of Joseph. My heart ached all day as though it were being stabbed. Whenever I saw a trace of Joseph in anything, unbearable sorrow would strike.

My husband, who rarely cries, often wept when he felt the absence of Joseph. He cried so much I was afraid he would have a breakdown. Above all, I was stricken with the guilt that I had failed to protect my son. *I should have been there. If I had been there with him, I could have prevented this. Why was I not there to protect my son?*

I never took my eyes off Joseph when we went to the pool. And even though we went to the pool so often, I had never seen Joseph have a seizure in the water. As his mom, I couldn't protect and save him. His father, his teacher, and even the lifeguard—no one could rescue him. Now, Joseph was gone.

All the things I could have done for Joseph kept crawling back into my mind. During Joseph's childhood, I knew so little. Every single word I had thrown at him because of my pain and frustration came back to me like an arrow of regret piercing my heart. Joseph had to endure distant, cold gazes from the world for just being who he was. I deeply regretted that I had not embraced him and loved him more. Above all, it was unendurable to know that he had struggled in extreme pain and died alone—as if his lifelong fight hadn't been enough for him. It almost made me go out of my mind. I buried myself in these thoughts every single second of every single day. It even made it hard to breathe.

Life was strange. In those days of extreme mourning, when I couldn't even eat, sit still, or stand, I felt God pushing me to get up. The Sunday during the week of the funeral service was Thanksgiving Sunday in Canada. I sensed God pushing me to make sure my choir performed as planned. When I laid down, feeling empty, his voice prompted, "Sing praises." Even as my mind kept saying no, his voice continued: "Do it. I want you to do it." There was no way I could. I knew the choir members and the church would understand. To me, the sorrow had become torture, and disappointment turned to despair. I didn't understand, nor could I accept why God would tell me to sing praises when I couldn't even perform basic human functions. But this voice was so insistent I asked my youngest brother, Paul, who was staying with us after the funeral, in a faint voice, "God keeps telling me to perform with the choir on Sunday. What do I do? I can't do it …"

With a careful but firm voice, Paul responded, "Go. Do it, sister." He sounded so sure, but I pleaded again, "Do I have to?"

"The faster you stand up, the sooner you will be healed. You must get up no matter what, and I think it's better to start sooner rather than taking a few weeks."

Listening to his words, I felt a glimmer of strength enter

■ ■

my exhausted heart; I had to force myself to get up now or never.

"Yes, I should get up. I must stand up and give praise. If God wants me to do it, I have to do it."

So, on that Sunday, I conducted the Grace Church Choir and praised God with "But Thanks Be to God" from the *Messiah*. On Thanksgiving Sundays, it was customary to sing a song expressing gratitude toward God for giving us our daily bread. However, the song I had chosen for this year's Thanksgiving Sunday was about thanking Jesus for giving us victory through resurrection—a song more appropriate for Easter Sunday.

This too must have been in God's plan.

The music proclaimed: "But thanks, but thanks, thanks, but thanks be to God, thanks be to God, who giveth us the victory through our Lord Jesus Christ."

How ironic of the Holy Spirit to compel me to say, "Thanks be to God" during the time I felt most miserable and cut off from hope.

I remembered the days when I would run to choir practice, sleep-deprived because I had stayed up the night before wrestling with Joseph's seizures. Even in those days, singing praises was like sending out an SOS from someone lost in the ocean.

My Thanksgiving praise was offered in a much more desperate situation. I felt like I was breathing my last breath and making it a confession of my entire existence. I convinced myself, *This is my last resort; otherwise, I will die of sorrow.* I offered each song with every cell of my being. My only focus

■ □ ■ □ ■ □ ■ □ ■ □ ■ □ ■ □ ■ □ ■ □ ■ □ ■ □ ■ □ ■ □ ■ □ ■ □ ■ □

was the Lord Jesus Christ, who had risen from the dead to give us eternal salvation.

Only a few days had passed since I had lost Joseph. But even in such a short time, God demanded a song of thanksgiving from me. Yes, from me, a mother who had just buried a son in her heart forever.

Ever since Joseph passed away, my body and soul felt heavy, like a sponge soaked in water. Even singing praises didn't help much. My soul would be revived momentarily, but when I came home, I felt dead again. My life seemed like a rollercoaster—with endless ups and downs. Sometimes I would come alive for a second but immediately plummet to the depths of despair. Our daughter, Hannah, who worked and lived in New York, worried I was dangerously close to falling off a cliff. Instead of returning to New York after the funeral, she decided to stay with us.

Around that time, we remembered our annual family vacation, which we had been planning all year for the end of October.

Joseph had loved to travel with the entire family once a year. Since his siblings lived in different parts of the country, he would ask about them all the time. "How is Hannah?" "How is Esther?" Joseph was an expert in asking about other people. For example, when he saw missionaries whom he hadn't seen for many years, he would still remember their children's names.

◻ ◻

Usually, we chose a place by the beach for Joseph since he loved to swim so much. The year he died, we had booked a place by a beautiful beach and had already bought all our plane tickets. Our children had already booked time off work.

I couldn't imagine going on a family holiday without Joseph, so I asked my children for their understanding. "I'm really sorry, but I can't go like this."

After a few days, Hannah handed me a small picture frame as a gift. Inside the frame, the words read: "Count your blessings."

The words struck me.

I stared at the words, "Count your blessings," and I felt awakened.

I believed Joseph was a blessing, but so too were my four surviving children. God had blessed me abundantly.

Once this realization fully set in, my heart cried out for my other children who were trying so hard to consider my feelings. I started to count every blessing God had given to me.

My first and foremost blessing was Joseph. He was the one who taught me the true meaning of "blessing." Even now, the reason I can live and share with others who are suffering is because of Joseph.

My second son, Samuel, is also a great blessing. Like other families with disabled children, I used to worry about our unique family environment negatively impacting my other children. As a child, Samuel enjoyed playing the piano and used to practice before he went to school. Joseph would often smack the back of Samuel's head and run away. Samuel had frequently left for school crying.

Observing them, I worried my children would have emotional problems due to the physical and emotional scars from Joseph. I worried especially for Samuel who had to take care of his older brother despite being the younger son. I couldn't help but feel sorry for him.

Despite my worries, Samuel grew up to be a well-adjusted young man. In fact, his words comforted us during the funeral service: "I'm blessed by Joseph. He will always be a part of my life; he will always be my older brother. I look up to him. My brother inspires me to be a better person."

Having a brother like Joseph must have been difficult for Samuel, but as a result, Samuel developed genuine compassion for people with disabilities. As he matured, many people encouraged him to study business management, but Samuel found helping others most rewarding. He studied psychology as an undergrad and went on to study Christian counseling at a seminary. Now, he is a pastor specializing in family counseling, serving at a small church in Seattle. He also counsels autistic children and at-risk teens.

God's amazing grace also shines through the other siblings, Hannah, Esther, and Christian. While growing up alongside Joseph, witnessing his seizures often brought them to tears. But they were never able to run to their mother for comfort as I was always preoccupied with Joseph. As a result, I hadn't done anything for my other children who studied music, film, and business, respectively. I couldn't even take care of them while they were on such arduous journeys.

In my absence, God looked after them. He gave them a

heart for family, their siblings, friends, pastoral staff, as well as people with disabilities. More than anything, I was grateful Joseph's disability never shamed them. When friends came over, they proudly introduced Joseph.

Counting these blessings one by one, I couldn't thank God enough for showering his grace on my children—making each of them grow and mature so beautifully. I realized my four surviving children were also my greatest blessings. I am a truly blessed person.

As I was reminded of this, I knew I shouldn't dwell in my despair any longer. I resolved to pull myself together and go on the family trip. This way, I could console my four precious children who had lost their beloved brother.

Even when I decided to go, my heart was still crying out in despair, but I made every effort not to show any tears. It had been a month since Joseph had left us.

10

Bearing Fruit

We traveled to Mustique—an island in the Caribbean considered to be one of the most beautiful places in the world. Before this trip, I hadn't even heard of Mustique and expected it to be just like the tropical locations I'd been to before.

Mustique was unique. To get to the remote island where we stayed, we would have to transfer planes multiple times. After we finally reached the customs office, I noticed in the center of the wall hung a framed Bible verse written in large letters: "For God so loved the world that he gave his one and only Son, that whoever believes in him shall not perish but have eternal life" (John 3:16).

Reading this verse, the words "eternal life" caught my attention. It made me think, *Joseph went to heaven.*

Until this point, I had not thought about heaven or eternal life very deeply. I hadn't even thought of heaven as a real entity but as a concept. To me, heaven was a place believers in Christ would go after death—somewhere far away from where we live now.

That's why the verse on the wall didn't particularly move me. I walked out of the office merely surprised to see a Bible verse in a public place; even countries founded on Christianity, such as the United States, no longer permit public organizations to hang religious symbols.

On that day, I still grappled with my emotions. *How am I supposed to hold back my tears for a week?* I had decided to travel with the plan of holding it together for the sake of our children. So I headed to our villa, hoping the time would go quickly.

Arriving at the property, the beautiful view struck me unexpectedly. The brilliant colors of the sky and sea—stunning, pure, and untouched—instantly charmed me.

I realized too that this beautiful location could potentially trigger extreme distress. The weather was perfect for swimming, which made me think of Joseph. Unable to let myself enjoy the sights anymore, I collapsed onto the bedroom floor and stayed alone in my room.

Whenever Joseph saw the ocean, he shouted in Korean, "Bada bara! Bada bara!" ("Look at the ocean! Look at the ocean!"), a phrase he had learned from my mother. In response, I would always say, "Yes, there is the sea." Then Joseph would run into the water, shouting, "Swimming, swimming!" These memories flooded my mind and drove me crazy. All I wanted to do was touch him with my own hands.

■ □ ■ □ ■ □ ■ □ ■ □ ■ □ ■ □ ■ □ ■ □ ■ □ ■ □ ■ □ ■ □ ■ □ ■ □ ■ □ ■ □ ■

Even though it felt like I could reach out and touch him, Joseph now only existed in my memory. Facing this cruel reality, I gripped my chest and continued to weep and mourn.

Joseph, you left me. I can't live anymore without you. I miss you so much. I can't live without you.

During this grieving period, I couldn't suppress my desperate longing for Joseph. The sight of the villa made it worse. Yearning for Joseph had become a chronic pain, which suffocated me. I was overwhelmed with deep regret over taking the trip. It seemed I could collapse at any moment from the insufferable grief.

Trying to relieve my sorrows, I suggested we hold a family worship service. During the service, we watched a video of Joseph shown at his funeral—a photo montage of his life.

Even after the service, my heart was still restless. As time went by, my mind gradually went from rocky waves to a violent storm. Being engulfed by this mental storm, I couldn't leave the room or fall asleep.

While everyone else slept, I threw myself down before God and prayed. I felt as if I couldn't live any longer without confessing what was on my mind. I fell to my knees and wailed, calling God's name.

God, why? Why did you take Joseph away from me so soon? Why did you have to take him when he was like a flower just beginning to fully blossom? I thought you could use Joseph and do your good work. So why did you take him like this? Why? Why in the world did you do it? If Joseph had lived just a month longer, he would have come with us on this trip and gone swimming. He would've had a wonderful time here. You couldn't allow him one more month of life? You had to let him suffer in pain. God, you promised me! Didn't you make me a promise through Jeremiah 29? A promise of a plan for Joseph, of hope for his journey and future? Where is that hope? It's over. Joseph is gone, and that hope doesn't matter. God, I don't have any hope now. Joseph is gone. No hope. There is no hope for me.

All the grief and resentment I had suppressed in my heart exploded. As if having a face-to-face confrontation with God, I moaned, questioned, and poured out my heart to God.

I exhausted myself. I tried to fall asleep, but to no avail. I got up and sat down again, when suddenly, I felt like I should read Jeremiah 29:11, which was given to me as God's covenant. In that moment, I needed to open the Bible and validate the meaning of the words.

As I looked at the verse again, the next verse after 29:11 caught my eye. "Then you will call upon me and come and pray to me, and I will hear you. You will seek me and find me, when you seek me with all your heart" (Jeremiah 29:12–13 ESV).

Upon being reminded of God's enduring promise, I fell to my knees once more. I confessed to God, crying and murmuring a prayer: *If this is true, God, reveal yourself to me tonight. I am about to die, unless I can see you. God, meet me, and show me Joseph who is with you now. Please show me Joseph just one more time. Please let me say good-bye.*

If anyone had been watching, they would have thought I was crazy. Maybe I was really out of my mind. I prayed,

prayed, and prayed again with a broken heart as if I would lose my senses unless I encountered God that night.

I don't know how long I prayed, but I must have passed out in mid-prayer sometime in the early morning. When I awoke (though it may have been in a dream), Joseph stood in front of me.

For a month, I had been praying to see Joseph, asking the Lord to show him to me even in my dreams. Finally, Joseph appeared before my eyes.

We were at Portal Alliance Church, the church Joseph loved the most and where his funeral had taken place—the setting of our last good-bye. Joseph stood in front of the chapel entrance, bright and healthy. Smiling broadly, he handed out the Sunday bulletins, a job he loved to do.

Next, I found Joseph standing in the chapel. I ran to him and gave him a big hug, not wanting to let go.

"Joseph!"

When I hugged him and touched his face, Joseph welcomed me with the brightest smile—the same pure and innocent smile that filled his face whenever he worshiped God.

This is all I had been yearning for throughout the past month. All I wanted to do was hug Joseph and touch his face once more. In this dream, I finally had that chance.

I woke up completely at peace; I thanked God immediately. *God, I see that my son now lives in heaven. I had always been seeking caregivers who would look after Joseph as well as I would. But now, Jesus (who is a thousand times better than I am) is taking care of him. Thank you, Lord. Now, I have no worries.*

□ □

I have been praying to see how he was, and you answered so faithfully. God, thank you. You are good. Thank you so much.

That's how God answered my prayers of seeing Joseph one more time. Even though we met in a dream, I had no doubt that I really had met Joseph.

This experience assured me where Joseph was and what he was doing. Because of this conviction, I woke up my husband and told him with a trembling voice, "Honey, I saw Joseph. I met him in my dream, and Joseph was so happy. He's in heaven, and he's happy."

↩

After seeing that Joseph was well, I awoke to a brand-new morning. The beauty of the island no longer induced sadness or guilt. I didn't need to feel sorry that Joseph wasn't able to swim at this beach. In fact, my confirmation of Joseph in heaven was lovelier than anything in the world. Now while enjoying the marvelous sunrise, I felt peace and, while resting under the sun, gratitude.

I could finally believe my parting with Joseph was not the end of our story; I would see him again soon. Just as a child may leave home to study in a foreign country, Joseph lived apart from me, and Jesus was taking care of him. Overnight, all my confusion, sadness, and grief transformed into hope.

Having this wonder in my heart, I asked one of the housekeepers whether there was a church nearby so we could attend Sunday service.

"Do you want to go to church today?" she responded. "Usually, when we have guests on Sundays, I have to miss Sunday service. But if you want to go to church today, I can attend the service with you as a guide. We have two churches near here. One church, my father is the pastor and the other one, my sister is the pastor. Which one would you like to go to?"

Her eyes sparkled when she gave me the details of church; she was clearly excited to attend with us. We suggested going to the church closer to our hotel. Excitedly, she disappeared for a couple of minutes and returned in a new outfit. On this sizzling hot day, she wore a formal dress suit and even a pair of gloves.

When we arrived at the church, thirty minutes before the service was to start, seventy to eighty people already packed the chapel. They seemed to be locals who worked on the island. Interestingly, the women were dressed formally, including hats and gloves. The men wore white suits and hats. Everyone sported their best clothes.

Other than a few fans, no air conditioning cooled the chapel; but the heat didn't seem to bother the congregation. They worshiped God wholeheartedly. Everyone sang with exultation; they clapped their hands loudly, and some even cried.

We sang for one hour. My knees began to hurt, so I quietly sat down and continued singing. In this moment, I felt something very hot begin to surround me. Did the congregation's passion overwhelm my soul? I sat down because my knees hurt, but instantly I felt as though everyone was praying for me. Soon, I heard a booming voice, loud and magnificent. It wasn't just a feeling; the voice really touched my ears, then my heart, and then my entire body.

"Blood of Jesus, blood of Jesus, blood of Jesus …"

Perhaps it was because I was in an African church. The voice spoke to me in English instead of Korean. The congregation was still singing, but what I kept hearing was the Holy Spirit's voice echoing, "Blood of Jesus."

I couldn't figure out where the sound came from—whether from underneath, from the side, or from above. Yet, as the voice surrounded my body, mind, and soul, I knew I was being completely covered with the blood of Jesus. In that moment, like lightning, the memory of the Scripture I saw on the wall of the customs office struck me. "For God so loved the world that he gave his one and only Son, that whoever believes in him shall not perish but have eternal life" (John 3:16).

All my life, I thought I believed in Jesus. Finally, I experienced that true faith can divide the bones and joints to penetrate and awaken one's soul. I saw the cross of Jesus. God loved the world so desperately that he gave his only Son to carry the cross and to pay for our sins. At that moment, I felt Jesus' blood anoint my head.

This blood saved me. Because of the blood of Christ, we were born again as his children and can live together forever in heaven.

Once I realized the price of this blood, I couldn't help but sob. But this time, my tears were different. They were no longer tears of sorrow and agony, but of gratitude, happiness, redemption. The Lord's overwhelming love touched my heart.

■ □ ■ □ ■ □ ■ □ ■ □ ■ □ ■ □ ■ □ ■ □ ■ □ ■ □ ■ □ ■ □ ■ □ ■ □ ■ □ ■ □

Above all, my eyes now saw Jesus' love when he took the burden of carrying the cross. All this time, I had only known John 3:16 as the fact that we can receive eternal life through the blood of Jesus. But on this day, I felt the burning love of a God who loved us so much he sacrificed his own Son.

What amazing grace! God demonstrated his love for us, to each of us, through the blood of Jesus.

Once I fully experienced this great love, I realized all my pains and worries meant nothing. After all, these problems rest within the boundaries of God's limitless love and grace.

Although Joseph was dead, he had gained eternal life though Jesus. And though I had to part with Joseph now, eventually, I would go to heaven to see him again through the power of Jesus' blood. I could now believe in all these things wholeheartedly.

What boundless hope this is! If God loves us so much that he has blessed us with eternal life, nothing can stand in our way. No matter what, God's love will claim us; no suffering or grief can take us down.

At first this family trip first had felt like death to me. But there, I experienced the baptism of the Holy Spirit and was covered by the blood of Jesus. I discovered my true reason to live.

Did God lead my family to this particular church on this particular island in order to give me this gift? If so, our plan to visit here must have been by God's design—he who knows everything and has impeccable timing.

I realized nothing was an accident. The way Joseph left and

the way I mourned had led us to this service at this church. I came to believe that everything was according to God's flawless plan and perfect control, to give us unswerving faith and peace.

Ever since that day the Holy Spirit enveloped my entire being, I clung to the gospel for my life. Jesus not only died for me but was also resurrected for me. And I shall receive everlasting life by believing in his precious blood. This is the Gospel. As I realized the Gospel's essence and power, a hope for heaven blazed in my heart. How precious is the good news that we can live guided by the Father on earth and then return to the Father's embrace and live forever with our brothers and sisters in heaven! This good news truly rejuvenated me.

Since then, something in my heart urges me to share the Gospel. I had never disregarded sharing, but once the kingdom of heaven became a real entity in my heart, rather than a theory, I couldn't sit still. I especially longed to share this good news with mothers raising children with disabilities. I urgently wanted to race against time to let them know about life in heaven where there is no night, no disease, no tears, no raging sea, and where everything shines like the sun.

A calling also arose to share the Father's heart, who loves children just like Joseph. After I was baptized with the Holy Spirit, this love of God became real and tangible to me.

God spoke to my heart: *Now that you know this love, you must go and love the least of your brothers and sisters. Share the Gospel and my love with them. Whatever you do for them is what you do for me.*

The day after I returned from the trip, I went to choir practice. The choir members, seeing my glowing face, asked if my trip went well. They could tell something was different.

I shared the story of what happened to me on the island. What could be better than tasting the love of the Lord in the presence of the Holy Spirit?

From that day on my husband and I acted quickly, rooted in the hope God had bestowed on us. One of our major missions was to refocus on the business of Joe's Table, a coffee shop we had started in March of that year but had been placed on a temporary hiatus. We had developed Joe's Table so Joseph, and others with developmental disabilities, could have a career. Because Joseph enjoyed meeting people, we thought working at a coffee shop would make him feel happiest and most valued.

However, when Joseph left so suddenly in September, I had fallen into deep despair and thought my life was over. The Bethesda mothers later told me they worried that since Joseph was gone, I wouldn't want to see the Bethesda children again as they would remind me of Joseph. They worried I would avoid them.

God thought otherwise. He put a new heart in me. Now, the Bethesda children feel like my own. Before, I only had Joseph in my heart; but now, I embrace these children as my own.

So has my husband. Since Joseph left, he has poured out his whole heart for the cause of helping people with disabilities as if to complete the unfinished work of Joseph. Thus, with unified hearts, my husband and I embarked on the coffee shop business to create employment opportunities and promote independence for people with developmental disabilities.

For the first word of our coffee shop's name, we took "Joe" from Joseph, which is also slang for coffee. We picked the second word "table," because the "t" resembles a cross, followed by the word "able." So, "Joe's Table" means Joseph is able to do everything through the power of the cross.

Our employment policy is based on inclusive hiring; we hire individuals with developmental disabilities as well as individuals without disabilities. This way, everyone can work side-by-side.

In terms of our marketing strategy, we strive to win customers through taste and quality rather than sympathy. In this way, Joe's Table hopes to spread the spirit of inclusive employment to other career fields and businesses. Of course, running a system in which employees are hired equally has given us an increased cost of labor. Naturally, it is our responsibility as a social enterprise to create opportunities for all types of people.

For the interior design of the cafe, we tried to capture Joseph's spirit. Since, like Jesus, Joe enjoyed exchanging hellos and building relationships, we set up a communal table so people can sit together, just like Jesus and his disciples did at the Last Supper. We wanted our customers to sit together and ask each other, "Hi, how are you? What is your name?"

Joe's Table, which was conceived in prayer, finally came to fruition in Burnaby on June 23, 2013—Joseph's birthday. Many customers return to the store often because they love the cafe's welcoming atmosphere and enjoy the homemade pastries made with the best ingredients. Of course, many come back for a good cup of joe.

Keeping up the momentum, God has provided a way for us to open the second and third locations of Joe's Table in Korea. Ultimately, we are overjoyed that through the opening of these locations in Korea, individuals with disabilities are given the opportunity to work for a living.

Our goal while continuing this work is for God to rejoice in our efforts. We pray God will come and meet his children in their hard work. Also, we pray that people who smell Joe's Table's coffee can also sense the fragrance of Jesus Christ. The dream we had for Joseph to be a missionary was thwarted due to his sudden death, but we pray this dream will live on. Through Joe's Table, Joseph fulfilled his calling as a missionary and has brought light to the darkest corners of the world.

We envision Joe's Table's expansion in South Korea, the United States, Canada, China, and even in North Korea where our brothers and sisters live, and furthermore, to the ends of the earth as Jesus commanded us. We are presently planning to open Joe's Table in the Billy Graham Library in Charlotte, North Carolina. We want Joe's Table to become a workplace for people with disabilities to realize their dreams and to become a place of comfort where we can share the message of the love, forgiveness, and reconciliation of Jesus Christ.

If Joe's Table reaches the entire world, I believe Joseph will be happy in heaven seeing his friends use their skills. He will praise and give glory to God for using him like the kernel of wheat that falls into the earth and bears much fruit.

Rising Up

Hi, Joseph, Mom's here. How are you?"

A few days ago, I visited Joseph's grave to say hello. When Joseph was alive, he was always the first person I'd go and see after a long trip; I would give him a big hug and ask him how he was doing. Even now, my feet want to take me to Joseph's room when I return home from a trip.

The only thing that's changed is I don't hear his voice, no matter how loudly I call for him. Although I miss him more each day, I cannot even hear an echo of my son's voice. So to fill the void, I sing next to his headstone all the songs we used to sing together.

"While the Lord is my Shepherd, and I'm kept in His care, like a lamb, dear and precious in His sight."

As I begin to sing this song, I recall how the Good Shepherd led Joseph on earth, then I am reminded of how happy Joseph is in heaven.

□ □

While I sing, my heart fills with hope for heaven. It makes me want to sing my favorite hymn continuously:

Just a few more days to be filled with praise,
and to tell the old, old story;
Then, when twilight falls, and my Savior calls,
I shall go to Him in glory.
I'll exchange my cross for a starry crown,
where the gates swing outward never;
At His feet I'll lay ev'ry burden down,
and with Jesus reign forever.[*]

Joseph taught me that a door between life and death waits for each of us to go through. Life in this physical world flashes by. Therefore, we should live a life of preparation for when the Lord calls us. He inscribed on my heart that life on earth isn't anything more than preparation for eternal life in heaven.

Standing before my son's grave, I can't help but lift up praises to the Lord. God's love pierces our hearts—and I've become more determined to live for the sake of this love and to make this love known to the world.

My swollen, tear-stained eyes were transfixed as I looked up at the blue sky to find Joseph's face between the clouds. I saw him smiling gently at me, waving his hand.

My friends are often worried about me and ask, "Are you doing all right?" I tell them it's true I miss Joseph more every

---

[*] George M. Gabriel, "Where the Gates Swing Outward Never," 1917.

■ □ ■ □ ■ □ ■ □ ■ □ ■ □ ■ □ ■ □ ■ □ ■ □ ■ □ ■ □ ■ □ ■ □ ■ □ ■ □ ■ □ ■ □ ■

day. But the more I miss him, the more I put my hope in the kingdom of heaven. So, even my longing for him feels like a blessing.

I believe I am now living the most blessed days of my life through Joseph. Since Joseph left so suddenly, I've come to know each day is priceless and cannot be bought with mere millions. That's why, these days, I lift up a prayer of gratitude first thing in the morning.

Thank you Lord for giving me a new day. Today may be the last day I live on this earth. So, Lord, help me live today to my best, glorifying your name. Teach me to live as a daughter of God who brings you joy.

As I open each day with this prayer, a thought enters my mind: *What will Jesus tell me when I enter the gate of heaven to meet Joseph? Will he say, "My good, faithful daughter, you've worked hard," and give me a crown? How would God feel if he saw me in heaven right now?*

Because of this, the kingdom of God and the heart of God have become the two most important priorities in my life. What has transformed me? I was once so selfish and faithless!

The secret is Joseph. From his birth to his death, Joseph told me God's message. Many mothers may also feel raising children has helped them know the heart of God.

Whether I'm on my way to early morning prayer or in the middle of a Bethesda meeting, I try to open my eyes and ears to the Lord. I want to listen to his message of embracing all children with disabilities, because when I do, I am full of joy. It is written that children are gifts from God; I discovered that, in place of Joseph, God has gathered and blessed my husband and me with a heart for many more children.

Today, once more, I am wiping away my tears. Counting my blessings, I live my life as someone who has received an undeserving gift. Because of Joseph who revealed the master plan of God, and because of many suffering children who will deliver other messages of God to me, I am rising up again to continue this blessed journey.

In May 2017, a special unit was opened in the Surrey Memorial Hospital for youth from ages six to seventeen with mental challenges. This unit is known as CAPSU (Child and Adolescent Psychiatric Stabilization Unit). My husband and I had the opportunity to provide some funds for this much-needed unit. This lounge has been named Joseph Chung Family Lounge.

I continue to praise God for being so merciful by giving us his only Son, Jesus, because he loved us so much. And I praise God for his abundant love, for being a Shepherd to all suffering children in the world.

About the Author

Dr. Stephanie Chung obtained her bachelor of music degree at the Seoul National University. She continued her studies in the master's program in piano at the University of Southern California, Los Angeles. Recently she had an honorary doctorate degree in humanities conferred on her by Trinity Western University.

Stephanie's contributions through music and philanthropy are evident in the numerous charitable events, fund-raisers, and concerts she has organized and at which she has performed. She is currently the director and conductor of the Vancouver Zion Mission Choir, a group of 160 Korean Canadians who have dedicated their lives to spreading joy and harmony globally through music. Stephanie has led the choir at the Palace of the Korean President in the Blue House in 2010. She was also featured as the main pianist at the Canadian Parliament Prayer Breakfast in 2010. In October 2011, the Zion Choir was honored to perform at Carnegie Hall in New York.

While Stephanie has been passionately pursuing her love for music, she has also been actively involved in the diplomatic community. Her credentials include her post as a former vice president of the Vancouver Consular Circle. Stephanie is also the ambassador of GAiN (Global Aid Network), "demonstrating the love of God, in word and deed." Through these posts, she always seeks ways to improve the welfare of people around the globe by demonstrating harmony and love.

In addition, Stephanie serves on numerous educational boards. In 2008, she became a board member for the Vancouver International Song Institute (VISI). She is also the founder of Bethesda Parents Society, a support group for Korean mothers and fathers of mentally handicapped children. Through the Bethesda Parents Society, Stephanie supports and educates women and men who have autistic children. She also served on the board of directors of the Vancouver Opera.

Stephanie is the founding director of Amenida Seniors' Community, which provides affordable, independent, and assisted living services to seniors in a truly multicultural environment. Amenida Seniors' Community is the only facility in British Columbia that fulfills the unique needs of Korean seniors by providing culturally specific meals and activities and bilingual staffing. It is filled with more than sixty Korean seniors and sixty Canadian seniors. Every day, there is a wide variety of opportunities for everyone to enjoy individual or shared activities and events.

Stephanie's most recent accomplishment is the establishment of Joe's Table Cafe, which is staffed with people with different abilities. Her vision for this venture came from her desire to find meaningful employment for her late son, Joseph

Chung. Joseph was diagnosed at a young age with autism and was also afflicted with seizure disorder. Since he always loved to socialize in his own loving and harmless way, Stephanie envisioned a job for him as a greeter to the patrons. In September 2012, however, Joseph passed away unexpectedly in a drowning accident. Nevertheless, Joe's Table continued to evolve and had its grand opening on June 23, 2013. Now it is a one-of-a-kind coffee shop that serves the community with the main focus of offering employment opportunities to those with different abilities. With the current location in Vancouver and two locations in South Korea, there are plans to open Joe's Tables across British Columbia and Canada in the months and years to come.

In 2014, Stephanie received the "Widen our World" award from Community Living BC for her work with Joe's Table Cafe. The award recognizes outstanding contributions toward creating environments that promote inclusiveness for people with differing abilities. Stephanie also received a service award from US President Barak Obama in 2013 and received the Order of Civil Merit "Dongbaek Medal" from South Korean President Geun-hye Park in 2015 for her contribution to promoting the rights and interests of Koreans abroad.

Stephanie Chung, a wife and mother of five, is a philanthropist at heart, an accomplished musician, a true diplomat, and an educator. She lives to generously give back to the world through her talents and loving heart.